QUIVERTREE
PUBLICATIONS

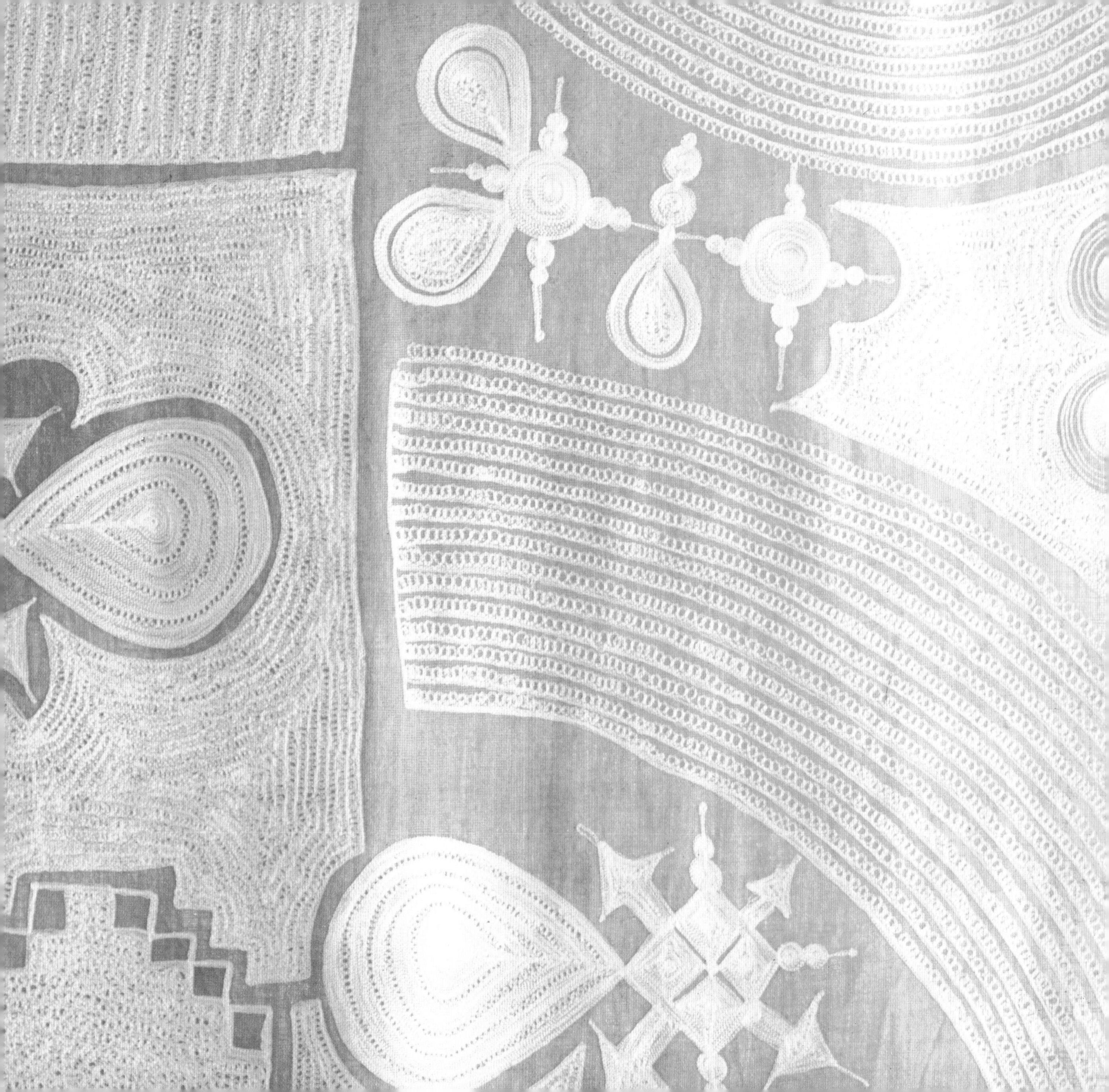

THE NEW SAFARI

design | decor | detail

PHOTOGRAPHS CRAIG FRASER **I** **WORDS** MANDY ALLEN
COPY EDITOR ROBYN ALEXANDER **I** **DESIGN & PRODUCTION** LIBBY DOYLE

introduction

In recent years there has been a proliferation of new safari lodges in southern Africa, enticing more and more visitors to include the untamed wilderness as part of their journey to this beautiful part of the world.

One of the most exciting evolutions in the industry has been a fresh definition of the term Safari Style. Gone are the conventional rustic and overtly colonial-style offerings we've come to expect. Instead, materials and objects (some traditional, some contemporary) are being rethought, reworked and reinterpreted, resulting in architecture and interiors that are both site-appropriate and exhilaratingly original.

Being on safari is no longer solely about the variety of game you manage to spot. Rather, it has come to be about experiencing a total lifestyle; one that incorporates unparalleled comfort, fine cuisine and a heightened connection with nature.

The camps and lodges included here have been selected for their pioneering spirit and dedication to creating a safari experience beyond the ordinary – a shared passion that finds expression in innovative architecture, design, decor and detailing. Regardless of whether they display an organic bent or possess ultramodern sensibilities, each of these lodges has been designed to offer a memorable, life-enriching adventure that touches the soul.

The destinations featured in this book are also at the forefront of the task of defining a new African design language. Each of them explores and reflects the huge diversity of styles that our continent has to offer and translates these into a sophisticated aesthetic that, while displaying a global sensibility, is still distinctly – and proudly – local.

It is thrilling to watch as new ideas are constantly being added to this original, 21st-century African style. What is depicted on the pages that follow is a carefully selected (although by no means definitive) collection of exceptional lodges that are part of this forward-thinking design movement. This is the New Safari.

CRAIG FRASER
Photographer and co-founder, Quivertree Publications

contents

foreword

Emerging in the last decade and a half, the New Safari style is significant in that it's a product of two extremes, of a creative, cultural synergy which in many ways is what contemporary South African society is all about. The safari design aesthetic has uniquely yoked hi-tech, high-end architecture with traditional low-tech African craft and fused them with an extremely original, courageous, soulful and sensitive – even sexy – interior design execution. It's an inspired surge of design that will be seen as a turning point in South Africa's design identity, and may even come to define it. Apart from a slew of great and tuned-in architects, designers and product developers, the New Safari couldn't have happened without the liberation of this country in 1994. Nor could it have happened without the platform of sound conservation standards and principles which have allowed the flourishing development of safari lodges and consequently a safari design discipline.

But, to go back 20 or 30 years, or more, New Safari implies that there was an old safari. There was, and it was the stuff of black-and-white photos, of hunting parties, gun oil, mosquito repellent and paraffin stoves. The old safari was all about action, an old-school endeavour of bushwhacking, shooting, living out roguish fantasies, and more or less camping in thatched rondavels on iron beds under scratchy blankets miles from nowhere while hyenas sniffed at the threshold. The point is that there was no decor look to the old safari. It was all about the event. Great camps existed and became legendary for their extravagant service.

Mala Mala was the zenith of safari destinations in the 1970s, but for all the charm of its bush setting, among the tableau of trophy heads on the walls was cane furniture that could have come from any ordinary holiday home. Design inspired by the magical concept of being in the African bush is as new as the celebration of place itself. African-inspired lifestyle products are now so firmly sewn into the fabric of our daily domestic existence that it's a wrench to recall a time when empty ostrich eggs were not used as light fittings and bowls, when curvy antelope horn wasn't used for door handles, chandeliers or table legs, when dressing gowns weren't available in khaki Italian linen and when 'vlei mud' body polish didn't come in a pump-action dispenser. The new safari is so hot, it's even come to town, but it all started with a demand for detailed, site-specific design for safari lodges.

The New Safari, as it is understood right now, is a look. Specifically, a look that provides a stage for the luxury leisure activity of being on safari. Luxury has played a vitally important role in the incubation of the New Safari style because without a certain standard of hospitality to attain, the challenge to create a dramatic and primal African aesthetic wouldn't have been so potent. Designing for the luxury market, too, allows an element of epic extraordinariness to emerge, one made all the more remarkable if that element is made of wood, stone or fossilized dung. Kudos then to the owners, developers and designers of the lodges, who raised the bar some 15 years ago and set the standard for this design stage in the first place.

When did New Safari begin? There was certainly a radical design aesthetic to the glass box villas that were built at Phinda in the early 1990s. At a time when most other lodges provided internally oriented accommodation, these brought the outside in and provided shocking intimate visual exposure to animals, bugs, light, stars, and… well… Africa. Then, when Singita Ebony was unveiled, it established a design language that had irresistible pull for a traveller to Africa. It provided moody drama, antiques, mystery, nostalgia, style and dressiness, the glamour of a Hollywood set and grand wood, glass and grass architecture in a thicket of huge canopy trees. This was thoroughbred style. But the design look was still a narrative interpretation of safari style. Singita Boulders – which opened shortly afterwards – saw a far more pointed approach to contemporizing the available African aesthetic. The result? The first organic, modernist interiors in the bush which, to their credit, remain iconic to this day. That, in my opinion, was the start of the New Safari proper. Why? For the first time indigenous materials like wood, stone, mud, iron and others found on site were interpreted and adapted to fit a relevant function, that wasn't a fantastical African folly. Purpose-designed furniture too was created to display both an edgy now-ness of form and ancient handling of materials, or vice versa. The undulating curve of a kudu horn was used as a door handle, for instance, but taking the idea further, timber from the site was used to create rustic but refined four-poster beds, which looked like smart rafts anchored in front of a vast game-viewing window. In time, this instinct in our designers for adaptation and interpretation has seen the development of traditional textiles such as mohair into super-innovative and fresh-looking forms of the material. Where mohair was once limited to blankets, for example, it is now commonly used in a very ropey, skeined form as upholstery. Felt, too, has lost its school-project stigma in the New Safari style and is the covering for enormous pebble-shaped cushions.

The rest is not only history, but thankfully brilliantly presented here in this book. Visually, it's a robust and sensual spectrum that documents the most evocative elements of the architecture, the interior design, and the handcrafted aspects of the best-designed lodges at this time. In the text the designers and architects provide insight into their motivation for the look and concept of each lodge, and what swiftly emerges is an intelligent, inspiring and accurate book about the spirit and sophistication of southern African safari design.

LIZ MORRIS
Editor, *Condé Nast House & Garden*

Singita Lebombo

Singita Lebombo exists as a delicate and almost invisible form in what many refer to as the Kruger National Park's most spectacular area. Set on a long, elevated site in the southeast region with aspects across the rolling Lebombo mountains, wildlife-abundant savannah and Nwanetsi river, the lodge is arranged in a succession of 15 private lofts and a public pavilion that clasp the side of the cliff like eagles' nests. Modular structures fashioned from simple materials – glass, steel and wood – are devoid of familiar architectural associations, the large vertical planes of glass exploring the idea of a boundary-less space and affording the privileged visitor dramatic encounters with both heaven and earth.

SINGITA LEBOMBO TAKES ITS CUES FROM NATURE'S FINEST ENGINEERS
THROUGH A DESIGN CONCEPT INSPIRED BY THE
POSITION AND STRUCTURE OF NESTS, DENS, EYRIES AND LAIRS.

SINGITA LEBOMBO 17

Singita Lebombo stands as the revolutionary tour de force of contemporary safari style. The jewel in the crown of the Singita group, Singita Lebombo successfully deviates from the bush boutique hotel vernacular with an architectural approach that goes beyond the traditional ideas of the built environment. In a similarly freethinking manner, Singita Lebombo's interior design, rather than tying itself to the African past, confidently explores an African future.

'We wanted to communicate an awareness of dwelling between the earth and the sky,' explains Andrew Makin of OMM Design Workshop who, with partner Janina Masojada and regular collaborator Joy Brasler as well as Boyd Ferguson, was responsible for the architectural direction of the lodge. 'The customary way of making an environment that respects its place in the African wilderness is to dig in and make it heavy with thatch, earth walls, screed floors. Our approach was to explore other non-physical, ethereal components of African consciousness.' As well as responding to the cliff-face location, the team's inspiration was the animal-made shelter and the manner in which nomadic people would set up temporary camp on the African plain. Glass plays a pivotal role in achieving the architects' aspirations of creating a sense of fluidity, transparency and impermanence. With the exception of the *sala* (outdoor pool pavilion) with its undulating changing-room wall, the structure has been limited to the most basic geometric form: steel-framed glass cubes are bolted to the cliff face and appear in the landscape as floating platforms. These glass boxes have been wrapped in 'shawls' of woven saligna-gum twigs that dapple the light and impart the effect of sleeping under a canopy of trees. The architecture allows for an astonishing degree of exposure to the immediate environment while still providing all the practical advantages of protection, comfort and privacy. Because of the transitory nature of the project – the owners have a 20-year concession on the land and are obliged to return the site to its natural state when it ends – the building was designed so everything could be disassembled and removed in a matter of weeks.

If the architecture of Singita Lebombo is revolutionary, its interior design has been nothing less than trendsetting. The work of Boyd Ferguson and Paul van den Berg of Cécile & Boyd's, who were pivotal to the conception of Singita Lebombo's look and feel from the outset, the decor integrates the urban and the organic, the sophisticated and the rustic, the hi-tech and the handcrafted. The tone is set by a largely neutral, sun-bleached palette that makes the already airy space seem even lighter and more diaphanous.

Like the architecture, the interior elements evoke the sensation of being close to the outdoors at all times: in the dining room guests experience the crunch of gravel underfoot; tea-light holders are made of ostrich egg shells; the shades of hanging lamps mimic the form of weaver nests; tactile wool rugs reference the dry bush grass; and round ottomans in the public lounge bring to mind the large boulders that flag the banks of the Nwanetsi. All this earthiness is contemporised by a selection of sleek, modern pieces, such as dining tables by South African furniture designer Haldane Martin. And to add a subtle hit of glamour, Ferguson has installed clear glass floor-standing lamps of his own design that when lit at night 'are suggestive of a bush fire,' and during the day take on the form of 'ice or falling rainwater.'

The 750-square-foot guest suites are decorated in the same style as the public spaces, with the addition of a series of gauzy drapes and heavier curtains that allow occupants to configure the bedroom, sitting room and bathroom spaces as they prefer. 'This, in combination with the glass, low-level furniture and *latte* screens,' says Paul van den Berg, 'makes it literally feel like you're camping under the stars.'

Vumbura Plains

Vumbura Plains Camp

Botswana's varied, still largely unspoilt habitats and remarkable profusion of wildlife have long held those seeking adventure in their thrall. Close brushes with nature are the order of the day at Vumbura Plains Camp, which is set among the wild fig, sausage and jackalberry trees in the extreme north of the Okavango delta. The private and public zones of this clean-lined structure have been constructed as a series of platforms, raised off the ground, and linked by a series of tree-lined boardwalks. Being lost in awe is a routine experience for visitors here, where the views of the vast delta flood plains and scenes of graceful lechwe quietly grazing provide memorable spectacles.

THE DESIGNERS OF VUMBURA PLAINS CAMP HAVE GONE BEYOND THE TRADITIONAL
AFRICAN VERNACULAR TO CREATE A PLACE OF SIMPLICITY AND RESTRAINT IN WHICH
GUESTS ARE INSPIRED TO MEDITATE ON THE WONDERS OF NATURE.

North meets South in more ways than one at Vumbura Plains Camp, a concession operated by Wilderness Safaris located in Botswana's Okavango delta flood plains. Vumbura is sectioned into two separate but lookalike sites: Vumbura Plains North, consisting of six twin-bedded chalets and one honeymoon suite, and Vumbura Plains South, which incorporates four twin-bedded chalets, a honeymoon suite and two family chalets. Each chalet has its own pool, viewing deck and *sala* (outdoor pavilion) and both camps feature a communal area for dining, indoor and open-air lounging, and game viewing. The sunken outdoor seating area with a fire pit is the place to be as the night settles in.

The North/South paradigm is also evident in Vumbura Plains' visual language, a sensitive exploration of contemporary lodge design that blends Scandinavian-style restraint with an exciting new African aesthetic.

The unobtrusive buildings utilise blonde sandblasted pine – bleached even whiter by the sun – as the primary construction material with virtually no additional materials (other than thatch and *latte* ceilings, canvas and mosquito-net 'walls' and bamboo blinds for protection from the elements) to interrupt the graceful and minimalist overall profile. Other components that resonate with functional eloquence include the modular built-in seating that replaces the usual sofas and armchairs, an emphasis on purity of form, a lack of superfluous detailing and an abundance of natural light.

Though Vumbura Plains does not draw on any familiar colonial or traditional African styles, its architecture, colour scheme and decor firmly locate it in its setting by continually referencing nature. The delicate palette of soft greens and blues, taupe and elephant-hide browns and greys are subtle reflections of what appears in the landscape. Organic shapes and forms also take all their cues from nature, including the boulder-like central bar counter sculpted from African mahogany, clusters of raw logs used as coffee tables and pebble-inspired ottomans in the suites and library. Almost every item was custom-designed by the creative team – a group headed by pioneering husband-and-wife architectural duo Silvio Rech and Lesley Carstens, together with George Boorsma and Lisebo Mokhesi of Ink Design Lab, and with the contribution of interior designers Laurie Owen and Carol English.

In order to amplify the indigenous craft/nature connection in a way that remained subtle, the team introduced a selection of commissioned objects: a feature chair handbeaded in a ring design and bearing the watery colours of the delta islands; calabash lights, white fish-leather cushions and fish leather-framed mirrors in the tents; handtufted cotton and leather rugs in the library and bedrooms; hanging egg-shaped chairs in the lounge; a cluster of tall sisal sculptures in the dining room that mimics the profiles of the area's termite mounds; and, suspended above this, an installation of resin lights moulded from the pods of sausage trees.

The rounded contours of the furniture soften the sharp geometry of the building, the rawness of the wood has been countered by the shine of copper and handblown glassware, and tactile fabrics lend an inviting softness to surfaces.

Unimpeded indoor-outdoor contact is the focus of each tented suite. Mosquito-net panelled 'walls' and sliding panels of shade cloth replace the customary glass, while kiaat vanities extend through each structure to the outdoor shower area to further blur the boundaries. The resin basins bring to mind the lily pads of the delta. A series of white screens of varying opacity allows one to configure the space for splendid isolation or open-plan airiness. In yet another homage to nature, one of these screens features a laser cutout pattern inspired by the large leaves of the surrounding flora. The same leaf motif is repeated on the white concrete shower tray – a delightful decorative flourish in an otherwise unadorned decor scheme.

One of the most strikingly modern aspects of the suites is their seamless, modular quality. Pine flooring extends upwards to compose the bed base, headboard and a desk as well as downward into the recessed lounge area to form both the floorboards and a built-in seating section.

'An essential aspect of the design process for us,' explains architect Silvio Rech, 'was to distil the essence of what it means to be on safari. As human beings our concept of the safari has evolved from hunting the Big Five to an excitement at the prospect of seeing the Big Five. This has ultimately given way to a new sensibility of simply being in and appreciating nature.' With its overriding sense of calm, Vumbura Plains Camp is the perfect location in which to do so.

PLANET BAOBAB

Planet Baobab

It's humbling to learn that the average age of the 17 baobab trees that give Planet Baobab its name is an astonishing 4 000 years and that the lunar-like landscape of the Makgadikgadi salt pans that border the camp cover the same area as Switzerland. In fact everything about Botswana's Kalahari desert region is awe-inspiring, from the diverse animal and plant species that it supports to the rich cultures of the indigenous people that call it home. Planet Baobab is situated along the dusty asphalt artery that connects Maun and Francistown, a place where cars come to a shuddering stop for passing elephants and the cracked, bone-coloured landscape is positively surreal. Instead of the splendid isolation offered by its more bush-bound counterparts, Planet Baobab evokes the welcoming bustle of a roadside pit stop in the middle of nowhere.

In a universe of safari lodges and bush camps with their refined decor schemes and demure palettes, Planet Baobab presents an entirely different proposition — a delightful Technicolor collision of ethnic pattern, traditional architecture and graphic African imagery.

Planet Baobab is not your average high-end safari destination. That's not to say it isn't accomplished in its design approach, that its services are anything but first-rate or that there aren't multitudes of inspiring ideas to uproot and incorporate into your own space. But its atmosphere, architecture and interior details dance to the beat of a different drum in a composition that is eclectic, refreshing and from the heart. Planet Baobab is unique in that guests can choose from several accommodation options, from huts fashioned in the local vernacular to offloading one's tent from the 4x4 and pitching it in a specially designated area.

The leisure opportunities here are equally diverse and include guided walks and quad-bike trips into the bush and salt pans with expert guides (only one path is used to prevent excessive ecological impact), overnighting under the stars, rubbing elbows at the shebeen (bar) with the locals and eccentric characters just passing through, or observing the elephants that lumber around at the nearby water hole.

As one of the founders of the Uncharted Africa Safari Co, together with partner Ralph Bousfield, Catherine Raphaely has directed the looks of all its camps – including the colonial-style classic that is Jack's Camp – to great acclaim. She describes the underlying design language of Planet Baobab as one that 'honours and respects the local culture.' The architectural simplicity of the structures – particularly that of the *en suite* huts characterised by thick walls, small windows and shaggy thatch to keep them cool – has been directly informed by the traditional building styles and materials used by the region's Kalanga people. So too the strong graphic patterning that adorns them, painted by the local women using mud and natural pigments obtained from charcoal, ash and termite mounds. While each hut is made unique by its own distinctive decoration, they are all punctuated by the same bright blue doors – a familiar local shade dubbed 'Botswana Blue' as it is the colour most often used to paint doors and window frames in rural Botswana.

Exterior spaces are based on the layouts of traditional *lelwapas* or meeting places. Although a basic simplicity of form underpins the architecture, it also displays distinctive elements of ornamentation. There are the abstract patterns that give texture to the floor of the shebeen, the quirky heart and cut-out circle shapes integrated into the squat walls and bench-like corner seats there, and the built-in beds and moulded open shelves in the huts, which are both obviously functional and beautifully sculptural.

First and foremost, the interiors have been inspired by southern Africa. Catherine Raphaely drew on 'the funky style of local shebeens and tuck shops and the creativity and ecologically correct approach to recycling of the townships and local villages' in creating the camp's feel-good look. Everything that catches the eye has a vibrant visual appeal: cheeky green beer bottle chandeliers; quilted, patchwork and crochet throws; cheap and cheerful enamelware; Coca Cola-tin-framed mirrors, retro cowhide-upholstered hoop chairs and woven and papier mâché bowls; vintage African movie and travel posters; and nostalgic black-and-white photographs from the *Drum* magazine archive. A handful of traditional pieces, such as elaborately carved *kgotla* chairs and rustic wooden day beds, further enhance the authentic mood. The potent African brew that is Planet Baobab is, quite simply, a tonic for the soul.

LITTLE KULALA

Little Kulala

So extraordinary is the location of Little Kulala in Namibia's Sossusvlei area that it might well have been art-directed by a set designer tasked with creating a primeval landscape on an unfamiliar if earth-like planet. Never-ending swathes of chalk-coloured sand segue into coral-red dunes, which in turn stretch into the Naukluft mountain range with its wide plateaus and deep canyons forged by ancient rainfalls. Nearby, the dry Auab riverbed winds its way to nowhere, flanked by preserved camel thorn trees that remain forever fixed in place like fossilised sentries. Though painterly because of its surreal quality, this is a landscape that is also remarkably alive, and its dramatic sunrises and sunsets tint the earth in shades from dusty pastels to fiery crimson. Awe-inspiring creatures as large as the regal oryx and as small as the toktokkie beetle roam the terrain, all adapted for survival in the harshest conditions. Even the delicate appearance of the indigenous grasses belies their ability to flourish through several seasons without water. Occasionally rain does fall; then the desert blooms briefly with a kaleidoscopic spectrum of flowers and plants.

FROM ITS SLIGHTLY ELEVATED POSITION, LITTLE KULALA DISCREETLY OBSERVES THE EBB AND FLOW OF LIFE IN SOSSUSVLEI'S SEA OF DUNES AND SAND, ITS ORGANIC CHARACTER AND RUSTIC DESIGN WHOLLY CONGRUOUS WITH ITS REMARKABLE SURROUNDINGS.

Even though the visitor to Little Kulala knows that what awaits is bound to be spectacular, one is still caught off-guard on arrival at the lodge. Architect Andy Chase has deliberately not granted any views of the dunes on approaching from the east in order to heighten the sense of anticipation and drama. It is only on moving through the massive front doors that guests are afforded their first glimpse of the breathtaking vista through a west-facing façade made up entirely of floor-to-ceiling glass doors. At the heart of his design concept was creating the impression of being in touch with nature 'but not overwhelmed by it, something that can happen very easily in this desert that is so huge and vast.' To this end the choice of location was critical and Little Kulala has been sited next to a dry riverbed with a scattering of trees in order to give visitors a more familiar, human sense of scale. 'This way,' explains Chase, 'nature can truly be assimilated and invited into the lodge wherever you are.'

A strong connection with nature is further suggested in the choice of principal materials – all sourced in Namibia. Walls were built using white cement and dune sand, which provides both texture and colour, while thatch was selected for its organic appearance as well as insulating qualities. Rather than opting for a slick geometric form, Chase designed the roof to take on an unrefined, slightly off-kilter look and introduced support pillars made of gnarled tree trunks – some of which 'grow' through the thatch – to further enhance the textural, rustic nature of the structure, as do the internal curved walls in the lodge's public areas. Of course, being located in a desert, practical requirements also determined some of the design choices, such as the ultra-deep wrap-around balcony of the main lodge, which provides shady respite from the unrelenting sun during the day. The deck is also used after dark for al fresco dining, the stars providing ethereal illumination. When not utilising the public spaces, guests make themselves at home in one of 11 luxuriously appointed canvas and thatch villas, each with an expansive bleached wooden deck fitted with a plunge pool.

Designer Laurie Owen created the welcoming look of Little Kulala's interior, an earthy organic style brushed by romantic and contemporary elements. Evidence of her overriding design inspiration – the Deadvlei region in the middle of the Sossusvlei with its dry, sun-baked character – is manifested in a colour palette consisting of bleached bone, mud and the faintest hints of silver and washed-out green. The furniture, much of it bespoke, is as curvaceous and undulating as the dunes outside: for example, the low-level pebble-like coffee tables, felt 'seed pod' floor cushions and ottomans (by textile artist Ronél Jordaan) and shapely mohair-covered loungers. Textures too are of the earth. Wool, felt, mohair, knotted leather, hand-dyed linens, raffia, roughly hewn wood, handmade beads, clay, paint (a traditional blend of sand and natural pigments) and handcarved sandstone are all tangible references to the distinctive beauty of the immediate environment. The organic connection goes deeper than mere aesthetics: many of the functional and decorative objects also have an ecofriendly bent, such as the fabrics utilised throughout, which have been coloured using only natural vegetable dyes; the recycled handblown glass vessels in the dining area; wooden floating shelves, furniture and light fittings (including the eye-catching twig chandelier in the main lodge) fashioned from alien plant species; and Zulu Mama chairs by South African designer Haldane Martin in the dining and lounge areas, which are made using recycled plastic. 'The mood and feel of this lodge is cool, serene, cocooning and slightly surreal,' Laurie Owen says. 'It's a slice of heaven in the middle of the desert.'

'Kulala' means 'the place where you rest or stay' in Oshiwambo, and one of the undisputed highlights of staying here is sleeping on the roof of your villa, which can be accessed via an internal staircase. With the rest of the world a million miles away and the stars in the inky southern sky shining bright, you'll quickly understand what she means. Heaven is indeed a place on earth.

Madikwe

MADIKWE SAFARI LODGE

Every visitor to Madikwe Safari Lodge will have his or her own defining 'bush' moment. For some it may come from catching a glimpse of a family of endangered wild dogs, tracking a pride of lion from an open-top 4x4 at dusk or the awe-inspiring thrill of observing a herd of elephant close up as they cool down in the mud of the nearby Marico river. For others it may be as simple as watching the sun rising over the Dwarsberg mountains or retreating to one's private deck to eavesdrop on the nocturnal sounds emanating from the plains that unfold into the distance. The lodge, with its rustic-hideaway quality, is located in the malaria-free Madikwe Game Reserve in South Africa's North West Province, a region boasting several richly diverse habitats that are positioned at the ecological junction between the bushveld and the Kalahari.

The organic and earthy design vernacular of Madikwe Safari Lodge serves as an entirely appropriate setting from which to feel — and answer — the call of the wild.

Like the gnarled leadwood, fig and bushwillow trees, grass-tufted koppies and crooked termite mounds so ubiquitous in the landscape, the adobe-style buildings of Madikwe Safari Lodge seem to have simply taken root and grown into place. As in nature, straight lines are nowhere to be found in the sturdily shaped structures fashioned from thatch, roughly hewn stone work and Cretestone-plastered walls that have been tinted in earthy colours, rubbed with wax, and 'toasted' with a blowtorch to lend notes of texture.

The layout of the lodge – consisting of three intimate camps totalling 20 suites with plunge pools, and a series of guest areas – eschews a traditional sequential arrangement in favour of a blueprint provided by the animal inhabitants of the land. 'Before beginning the design process,' explains architect Rob Marnewick, 'I spent a lot of time just getting a feeling for the site. I followed the old animal tracks to the places they used to rest at night. These nodes functioned as the animals' amphitheatres, where their backs were protected and they could look out. The positioning and layout of the guest suites – thoroughly screened from each other for privacy – and the public areas evolved from there. One experiences the building from the inside looking out, essentially like a series of verandas in the bush.' Also seemingly inspired by the idea of the animal shelter, a series of tucked-away niches in the public areas provide quiet spots to which guests can retreat.

An emphasis on sculptured organic forms and rustic materials serves to firmly place the buildings in the environment without impacting on it. Even the immediate surrounding vegetation has been left untouched in order for the man-made structures to fully connect with nature. Marnewick went 'bush shopping' to source most of his materials, including the dramatic leadwood posts that feature throughout the lodge. Over two hundred of these were reclaimed from the reserve's road- and facility-building projects and integrated into Madikwe's design. The sculpted forms of the buildings have been continued in the built-in vanities, slabs and fireplaces of the interiors; a practical consideration that also imparts a seamless quality to the spaces.

The interior, by Conservation Corporation Africa's creative director, Chris Browne, is a playful take on the traditional stoep (porch) culture so inherently associated with the Marico area, as it's known locally (one of its most celebrated former residents was the writer Herman Charles Bosman, whose preferred subject matter was his beloved bushveld). A warm interior colour scheme of pumpkin, oxblood red and terracotta holds its own against the robust architecture with opulent copper accents in the form of artefacts, *objets* and elements integrated into the building, such as the woven copper screens that separate the bedrooms and bathrooms. As with the majority of Browne's interiors, an easy-going mood prevails. Furniture tends to bear the patina of age and promotes the idea of informal lounging; an abundance of beanbags and cheeky woven banana-fibre chairs emphasise the laid-back message. The inclusion of pan-African craft correlates to the geographical location of the lodge, which is near the Botswana border. Another Browne signature, a measure of quirk, can be found in the decorative flourishes: for example, the iconic South African advertising for a well-known brand of tobacco, transferred onto scatter cushions as a handstitched motif and bearing the warning 'Danger: Smoking Kills'.

Though he could not have foreseen the emergence of the luxury safari catering to the extravagant proclivities of the contemporary global traveller, the Madikwe experience is little changed since Herman Charles Bosman penned these words: 'I have seen the moon in other places besides the Marico. But it is not the same there. It does strange things to you, the Marico moon, and in your heart are wild and fragrant fancies, and your thoughts go very far away.'

Hunter's Marataba

Hunter's Marataba

The Waterberg mountains unfold before visitors to Hunter's Marataba like ancient monoliths deliberately placed to provide a majestic backdrop to the untamed elements. The lodge is located in the heart of the Limpopo's Marakele National Park, an awe-inspiring landscape encompassing vast plains, dense bushveld, meandering rivers, deep gorges and towering rocky peaks. The area, in South Africa's northernmost province, is steeped in legend and rich with tradition and culture, having once functioned as a gateway for trade between the people of what are now the countries of South Africa, Botswana, Zimbabwe and Mozambique. This legacy of convergence is at the heart of Marataba's design vernacular, which comprises a meeting of ancient and contemporary African styles drawn from across the continent and expressed by a site-sensitive architectural composition of stone, glass and wood.

Privately owned by the Hunter family, Hunter's Marataba is rich with allusions to an African past and invites guests on a journey of the imagination. Stonemasonry is evocative of a great, long-lost civilization, spears and prehistoric currencies reference ancient traders, and iron and bronze artefacts pay homage to the artistry of the continent's craftspeople.

In designing Hunter's Marataba, architect Nick Plewman was challenged not only by a relatively complex site featuring low trees and thorn scrub with an aspect to the northwestern end of the Waterberg mountains, but also a client brief underpinned by an historically inspired narrative. 'The client's account told of an explorer arriving at the site to find stone remnants from a previous ancient dwelling, onto which he grafted his own settlement,' explains Plewman. It was this fiction that led to the design outcome: thick stone walls cradle each of the 12 luxury tented suites and substantial stone buttresses support an otherwise seemingly weightless main lodge, which is characterised by lofty spaces and constructed of timber and glass.

The buildings have been influenced as much by the client's directive as they have by the beauty of the natural environment and the stone was forged locally to ensure it fully harmonises with the surroundings. Plewman's purpose in laying out the main lodge was to embrace the magnificent views and the roofs have been pitched upwards to take in the mountain peaks and sky. Though relatively high-rise, the height of these roofs was carefully calculated to remain within the tree line. As a result, the building is almost invisible until one is right in front of it.

It is not only the extensive use of stone and glass that connects visitors to Marataba with the immediate environment, but also the various water features at its entrance, which serve as dramatic metaphors for Africa's life force and induce a feeling of calm. One of the more striking spaces in the main lodge is the library, which is housed within a stone tower and also features panoramic views of the scenery. References to countries further afield have been integrated into the architecture, such as the carved Zanzibari doors and windows used in the reception and guest areas.

The mother-daughter interior design team of Jill and Jacqui Hunter added their own layers of history to develop the explorer/African trade route theme, creating a style described by Jacqui as 'the ancient embracing the modern.' Low-level furnishings such as giant day beds, deep window seats, hammocks, oversized modular outdoor furniture, beanbags and bespoke long sofas and footstools set the inviting scene. The palette betrays the pair's strong attraction to the all-pervasive natural beauty of the region; colours morph from the fresh green of new grass and soft greys of water to the purples and reds so characteristic of the Waterberg, though crisp watermelon is an undeniably contemporary addition. Bronze alludes to the past and serves to link the spaces.

While surface interest abounds in the form of contrasting textures (cotton, velvet, linen and leather) and details such as beads, buttons, cocoa-bean chips and ostrich-egg shell, pattern is largely limited to what occurs in nature in the form of Nguni cowhides.

Local artisans have been widely employed in the creation of custom-designed pieces that range from bronze crocheted screens, lampshades and extraordinary beaded pendant lights to handmade crockery, wood and metal candlesticks, dining-room furniture (made of oak wine barrels) and handwoven bedspreads. In the process of developing Marataba's unique visual idiom, the designers have also introduced items collected from every corner of Africa including Tonga doors from Zimbabwe (used as tabletops in the bedrooms), Ghanaian Ashanti stools, Dogon beds from Mali, carved Baule figures from the Ivory Coast, metal currencies that are decoratively displayed, and traditional spears that are installed above the beds as well as being inventively used as towel rails in the bathrooms.

The overall effect, far from feeling contrived, is comfortable, authentic and irreproachably stylish.

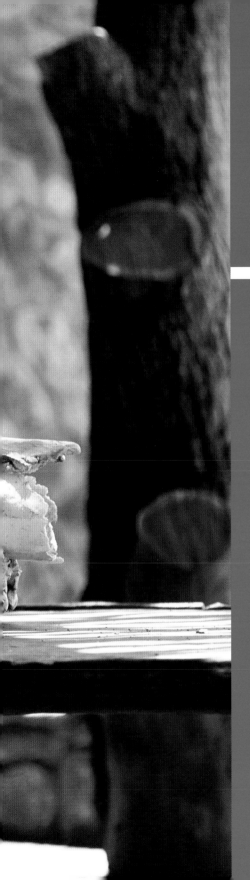

Singita Boulders

Singita Boulders

Singita Boulders Lodge both towers over the landscape and is etched into it; it's a monolith of curving thatch, grass-planted roofs and piled stone walls that merges seamlessly with the rugged topography of the Sand river. Like Singita Ebony, Singita Boulders is the product of a collaboration between architect Bruce Stafford and designers Boyd Ferguson and Paul van den Berg of Cécile & Boyd's. However, the two lodges – although they are only 10 minutes apart and share the Singita ethos of unparalleled luxury – could not be more different. While the visual idiom of Singita Ebony is anchored in the now-familiar colonial tradition, Singita Boulders has forged an exciting new design language that is at once organic and primitive, contemporary and sophisticated.

Singita Boulders' strong visual impact is largely a product of its rough-edged circular forms and interiors that maintain the earthy spirit of the architecture. This is design evolution made tangible.

There is not a straight line to be found at Singita Boulders, which is set in the heart of the Singita Private Game Reserve. The site is characterised by rocky outcrops overlooking the banks of the Sand river and the plains beyond. This directly informed the notion of a lodge that had been carved out of the earth, one that conformed – quite literally – to the lay of the land. 'The concept for Boulders speaks to the very heart of what it is that people love about being in the bush,' explains Paul van den Berg. 'You want to sit around a fire under the sky with your hands and feet buried in the sand, to truly feel grounded. Boulders is truly grounded.'

The structure, composed of 12 suites accessed by raised walkways and a central public area, has been engineered into the side of the riverbank with only parts of it being elevated to take advantage of the views. Even the interior architectural features – such as walls, steps, fireplaces, shelves and counters – feel as if they have been sculpted out of rock rather than conventionally assembled. So rooted in the earth is this lodge that a section of the construction is partially underground, with a roof structure that has been planted with grass and designed to withstand the weight of the herds of elephant that occasionally lumber across it.

The predominant materials throughout are thatch for the roof, polished concrete and slate for the floors, and the packed stone that makes up the curved exterior and interior walls – all seemingly sourced directly from nature. Man-made glass also plays a role, acting like an invisible clip-on barrier to separate guests from the heat, insects and wildlife.

Continuing the notion that Singita Boulders has been carved out of the earth, much of the furniture is built in. The main living room is anchored by three imposing columns, with the central column featuring wrap-around built-in seating with leather cushions for comfort.

Texture intensifies the organic design philosophy and is present in everything from the architectural detailing (untreated balau decks outdoors and the main entrance hall floor that has been designed to resemble dried riverbeds) and textiles (mohair, raw silk, leather, hide, woollen tweed, grass fibres, pure linen) to decoration (rough-hewn Senufo artefacts, tree-root tables, Dogon benches, kudu-horn side tables, unframed bevelled mirrors, stone bowl-shaped basins, animal skulls, groupings of carved wood vessels and giant palm pots).

Colours too are of the landscape: bone, skin, mud, bark, rich chocolates, dusty greys. Beaten copper and bronze pay homage to indigenous ornamentation and unearthed artefacts, providing a low-key element of shine that never competes with the earthy, bohemian essence of the interior.

If the ritual of visiting the bush is the result of a need to bond with the earth, then Singita Boulders can be thought of as a raw, honest and naturally beautiful conduit to doing so.

Ngala

NGALA TENTED CAMP

Three kilometres from the Kruger National Park's Orpen Gate, in a dense thicket of jackalberry trees, a surprise awaits. Ngala Tented Camp remains true to its name by including six tented suites on raised platforms, but the accommodation also offers a sophisticated update on the tented-safari decor concept by merging modern Scandinavian elements with surprising accents of colour and retro memorabilia. The camp takes all its cues from the seasonal Timbavati river. Whether dry or full, the Timbavati provides the daily spectacle for guests, who can watch game wander by from elevated timber viewing decks or take a cooling dip in the lap pool with its contours that echo those of the riverbank.

HERE THE QUIRKY INTERIOR DESIGN MAKES LITTLE ATTEMPT TO REFLECT THE NATURAL LANDSCAPE.

INSTEAD, ALL THE OBVIOUS CLICHÉS HAVE BEEN AVOIDED WITHOUT FORFEITING COMFORT,

LUXURY OR THE TENTED-SAFARI EXPERIENCE IN ANY WAY.

Unlike other lodges, which shape themselves around the views provided by Mother Nature, the starting point for the layout of Ngala Tented Camp was informed by the shade of the trees. 'We wanted the camp to celebrate the wildness of the Timbavati river,' explains Conservation Corporation Africa's creative director, Chris Browne. 'But the cover on the riverbank was too thin, so we nestled the tents and guest areas in the rich green grove of jackalberry trees.'

The camp's structures have been designed to both conceal themselves in the environment and reveal its beauty. A large communal building faces the riverbank and features various viewing decks and a curvaceous infinity pool. Areas are defined by their levels: an intimate sitting room is suspended on top and looks out on the vistas below, a dining room takes up the middle level and the camp's shop and kitchen are set on the lowest.

The individual *en suite* canvas tents stand on raised saligna-wood platforms; each is supported by a central column and perimeter ring beam. These go beyond their obvious structural function of keeping the tents upright, lending them a sharply tailored architectural profile. 'We aimed to introduce a more contemporary canvas vernacular that was fresh and new, as opposed to the classic safari-tent look,' says Browne. This idea has been taken further by keeping the outer canvas in the traditional olive green, while the interior canvas is a contemporary shade of mustard. The tents open up completely at the front and rear to allow air to flow through, to enhance the feeling of space and to connect the interiors with the tranquillity of the scene outside.

The clean, modern lines of the structures meant that Browne could 'play a bit' (in his words) by introducing organic furniture shapes and a few kitsch, retro pieces. The element of surprise underlies Browne's architectural and design approach throughout and is also reflected in the use of dry-packed Phalaborwa stone to construct rustic feature walls in the bathrooms and open-air showers of the tents. Unexpected flashes of acid green – 'it sounds incongruous in the bush but the location and retro feel I was going for made it the obvious choice of colour,' explains Browne – create a connection between the public spaces and the private havens of the bedrooms as well as adding a glamorous richness.

The interiors throughout have the restraint of contemporary Scandinavian minimalism but are made approachable by the presence of printed silks, chenilles, woven wicker, leather and other textured ingredients. In the bedrooms a less-is-more approach has been taken, with the bed taking centre stage. The ultimate surprise, however, is to be found in the nostalgic memorabilia and *objets* that pay tribute to the Kruger Park's past. Dinky cars, collectible Kruger Park teaspoons set in resin, mosaic pictures above the bar, agate stones mounted on the walls and curio-style soapstone carvings are all intended to provoke nostalgic delight and hark back to the park as it was in the 1960s and 1970s.

Exeter Leadwood

Exeter Leadwood Lodge is a beautiful and very private oasis in the western part of the Sabi Sand Game Reserve. The lodge overlooks the confluence of the Sand and Mabrak rivers, where colossal granite boulders rise dramatically from the riverbed and ancient leadwood and jackalberry trees form canopies of shade for the impressive range of birds and wildlife that frequents this extraordinary habitat. The building is a contemporary architectural vision rich in texture and patina and is experienced as a series of planes, steps and levels – a device that serves not only to emphasise the views, but also to enrich the senses.

LEADWOOD LODGE BOASTS A TACTILE BLEND OF BOLDLY EXPRESSED AND CONTRASTED MATERIALS:

CRUSHED STONE, RAW CEMENT, DARK MERANTI WOOD, ROUGH GRANITE AND GLASS.

The Conservation Corporation Africa name has long been synonymous with distinctive structures that feel utterly at ease in their immediate environments, and for Exeter Leadwood Lodge the group turned to architect Nick Plewman. What he has created is a surprisingly sleek, uncompromisingly contemporary design that manages to 'remain sympathetic to the traditional bush lodge aesthetic while eschewing all of its clichés.'

In the public building a series of soaring spaces has been set on different planes to serve multiple functions: lounge, viewing areas, bar and restaurant. This unusual arrangement of space creates an atmosphere of sophistication and depth. The rest of the visual drama is achieved through the use of materials. Granite walls delineating the primary spaces make direct reference to the river bedrock. These are juxtaposed with more refined features of polished concrete, timber and glass, all of which impart feelings of lightness and modernity to this singularly confident construction. The double-volume nature of the spaces also 'maximises the openness of the buildings on the riverside, enabling an increased degree of intimacy with the surrounding woodlands, all without losing the notions of security and comfort,' explains Plewman. Region-specific thatch serves to make the building merge respectfully with its surroundings.

A discreet location and limited accommodation – there are only four suites – endear Exeter Leadwood Lodge to a privacy-seeking clientele. The suites as well as the main lodge fell under the interior direction of Câline Williams-Wynn, who has carefully selected the interior details to create a dialogue with the pared-down architecture. Her vision for the lodge stays away from traditional ethnic design elements, favouring contemporary colour combinations and glamorous decorative detailing instead. Rich browns are highlighted by vivid splashes of aquamarine or turquoise, and luxury finds expression in exotic fabrics such as crushed velvet, shot taffeta, heavyweight linen and silk, some embroidered with semi-precious stones and crystals. Pattern has been restricted to 'that inspired by local artists,' says Williams-Wynn, and only a small selection of indigenous *objets* – including painted and polished Bamileke and Ashanti stools – are used as display items.

Exeter Leadwood Lodge is unique, says Nick Plewman, 'because it eschews whimsicality in favour of a clear, unambiguously luxurious but thoroughly intimate experience of the wild.' In the individual suites, thatch, granite walls and large sliding doors create a rugged charm, but the feel is also reminiscent of an urban loft (a colour palette of cream, charcoal and cocoa reinforces this notion). Each suite features a centrally situated bed, desk/work station, sitting room and luxurious bathroom. The suites also have their own private decks with plunge pools and are optimally positioned so that their occupants can, as Plewman and Conservation Corporation Africa intended, concentrate on enjoying their superlative natural surroundings.

The Outpost is situated in the remote northern Kruger National Park, perhaps the most secluded of all the Kruger's territories. Its wild and uncompromised landscape is characterised by billowing sour grass, thickets of ironwood trees virtually impenetrable in places, regal baobabs, colossal granite rocks, vast flood plains and two of the region's most vital rivers, the Limpopo and the Luvuvhu, with their resident populations of hippo and crocodile. Rooms are perched high so as to better take in nature's spectacle, which at times – when the fish eagle cries and the earth finally cools down with an almost palpable sigh – seems to be the manifestation not of reality, but of a glorious dream.

Thoroughly contemporary in nature, The Outpost writes its own definition of
the 21ˢᵗ-century safari lodge vernacular. Its architecture and interior design
reinterpret the sophistication of a cosmopolitan boutique hotel and sympathetically
transplant this into an untamed and remote setting.

From the ground up, The Outpost deliberately eschews any preconceived notions of the traditional. This is immediately apparent on viewing the prefabricated main structure and 12 free-standing guest suites, all of which are both graphic and Spartan in profile. The sense of modernity is further exaggerated by their elevated state on solid stilts of steel – a decision motivated by the steep lay of the land as well as a desire to optimise views and **touch the earth lightly.** The encounter between materials has also been rendered in a thoroughly up-to-date way. Timber, canvas and stonework may be materials shared by the majority of safari lodges, but in combination with steel, slabs of polished concrete and galvanised sheet metal, it is the powerfully modern overall composition and not its individual elements that elicits admiration.

It is testament to the talents of its architect – Italian-born, South African-based Enrico Daffonchio – that The Outpost integrates so harmoniously into its environment. Despite its intentionally contemporary leanings the structure does not isolate itself from the natural habitat. Instead, its charcoal-grey façade and foldaway walls make the transition from man-made structure to untamed bush a virtually uninterrupted one, allowing for a full-on interface between inside and out. 'The lodge gives visitors a very intense experience of the views, sounds and perfumes of the bush,' says Daffonchio. 'The stimulation is so extreme that some visitors have found it too much. But the vast majority are thrilled by the absence of barriers to the natural elements.'

The principles of **sustainable architecture** guided Daffonchio's hand during the entire design process: from the strict regulation of construction activities, careful water management, effective sun-orientation in order to minimise energy usage and a natural air-conditioning system, to the decisions to build around the trees and raise the lodge on stilts for a minimum footprint.

The concept of The Outpost was that of its original owners (the lodge has since been sold to a small consortium), innovative boutique hoteliers Christoff van Staden and Peter Aucamp. Their striking interior design echoes the contemporary sentiments of the architecture. Colours were deliberately chosen not to mimic those of the typical safari palette, so punchy blues and chic greys (rather than time-honoured khakis, ochres and dark mahogany) anchor the scheme. These are punctuated by pleasant shocks of primary brights as well as light-to-medium browns more typical of European than African interiors. Very little pattern or texture has found its way onto flat surfaces, bar a scattering of handembroidered and beaded feature cushions and the modern Nguni cowhide cubes that serve as seating around a low-slung Beninese table. These, and the specially commissioned kiaat Tusk tables with their gently bowed legs that appear in the public and private spaces, are the only visibly ethnic artefacts. Furnishings – the large majority of them bespoke – are as sleek in their forms as they are sparse in their placement, a result of the designers' unwavering conviction that in the bush, less is more. 'We were inspired by our desire to set a new standard,' they explain. 'It was a challenge to prove that modern design can be compatible with a setting like this. The interiors were not intended to reflect the location. They merely enhance the location and serve to make guests aware of the space and views around them. Furniture and spaces are comfortable but functional. It is the opposite of self-indulgent.'

The Outpost is part of a 30-year lease granted by the indigenous inhabitants of the land, the Makuleke people. Currently the community benefits from part of the lodge's earnings as well as being trained in the ecotourism industry so as to effectively take the reins of this remarkable place when the concession ends.

Singita Sweni

Singita Sweni

Separated from Singita Lebombo by less than a kilometre, the six-villa Singita Sweni (the smallest of the Singita lodges) shares its big sister's diaphanous architectural sensibilities and directive to touch the earth lightly. Unlike Singita Lebombo, however, Singita Sweni does not perch high on a cliff, nor does it mimic Singita Lebombo's luminously pale, unadorned interior design. Instead it stands – cool and serene – on timber stilts set low on the dappled water's edge of the Sweni River, a recurring colour palette of khaki, muddied browns and fresh greens referencing and paying homage to the river and the lush euphorbia and fever trees that it nourishes.

SINGITA SWENI WAS DESIGNED WITH ECOLOGICAL PRINCIPLES IN MIND.
GLASS CUBES ENSCONCED IN NESTS OF WOVEN *LATTE* BRANCHES ARE MERELY TEMPORARY
STRUCTURES, ALLOWING VISITORS TO BEAR SILENT WITNESS TO AND
CONNECT WITH THE UNTAMED ENVIRONMENT OUTSIDE.

Shifting light is an ever-present feature in the spaces at Singita Sweni, the intentional end result of a structural concept that employs glass, steel and wood to address the conditions of the Elysian riverside site. A series of cubes elevated from the ground on timber stilts constitute the building, which is sectioned into a central meeting place, raised wooden walkways, dark timber decks oriented towards the views, and six exclusive suites each with their own lounge, dining area and pool. These glass cubes have been ingeniously 'wrapped' in woven *latte* screens that serve both to holistically integrate them into the vegetation and topography, and veil them in shade and preserve the privacy of Sweni's two-legged residents.

While there is a determined sense of modernism to the architecture, this is counterbalanced by occasional interruptions from nature, organic or otherwise: for example, the euphorbia trees that rise out of the viewing decks, their unrefined architectural forms creating living sculptures; and the dramatic interior feature walls in the public space (installed to partially conceal areas like work stations), which were fashioned from concrete, then distressed and highly polished to resemble smooth, weather-worn tree trunks. Even the fireplaces – created the same way as the concrete 'tree trunks' – appear to have been split down the middle by lightning (a design element shared with Singita Lebombo).

This is the second Singita project that was entrusted to architects Andrew Makin and Janina Masojada of OMM Design Workshop and Durban-based Joy Brasler, and united them once again with designers Boyd Ferguson and Paul van den Berg of Cécile & Boyd's. Like the architecture, the interior design direction was profoundly influenced by ecological principles, and like the architecture, it has been masterfully interpreted in a way that is site-appropriate but also luxurious, original and contemporary. African artefacts, ethnic artworks, earthenware pots, indigenous materials, leather and khaki take care of the 'safari' aspect, while urban comforts, modern finishes and elegant furnishings convey the other face of Sweni – an exclusive boutique hotel in the bush.

The designers have sought to connect the interiors to the landscape via Sweni's palette: a potent brew of mud browns uplifted by avocado, lime, olive and other leafy greens. The designers have also employed their signature inventiveness to create another subtle layer of interest. Open up the pale cream menu and you are greeted by a bright green sheet of paper; look into the pantry and you are met with a cranberry-red interior; or throw back the chalk-coloured bedcovers and recline on a vibrant orange sheet. 'We call it "hiding colour",' explains Paul van den Berg. 'Just as nature reveals its jewel-like tints subtly, so brighter colours surprise guests as they discover Sweni. It's like a bird that at first looks ordinary, but when it lifts its wings there's this shock of vibrancy.' In fact, uncovering all the details at Sweni is a veritable voyage of discovery. It's only when you look closely that you notice the floors and decks are made out of random planks of wood, and that the curtains in the bedrooms have been edged in leather and given an urban edge with stainless-steel rivets embedded into the fabric.

The focus of each villa is the low-rise floating bed with its cascading 'wall' of grey beaded curtains and mosquito-net 'tent'. The heavyweight textile curtains can be configured in different ways, to either open spaces up to the views or shroud them in privacy as the day draws to a close – effectively allowing guests to create their own architecture within their particular glass cube.

PHINDA GETTY HOUSE

Phinda Getty

Phinda Getty House sits unobtrusively in its tranquil setting, ringed by gently rolling hills and overlooking an extinct volcano now covered in lush vegetation. The lodge is situated in the southwestern region of the Phinda Private Game Reserve in northern KwaZulu-Natal. At 22 000 hectares, Phinda is one of southern Africa's largest conservation areas and features no less than seven distinct wildlife habitats, including a sand forest abundant with exotic tree-growing orchids, open savannah dominated by otherworldly acacia trees and an evergreen forest made lush with tamboti, sycamore fig and weeping boerbean trees. Unique to the portfolio of Conservation Corporation Africa's lodges, Phinda Getty House is intended as a sole-use villa for families or groups when its owners – as the name suggests, members of the famed Getty dynasty – are not in residence.

THE CHOICE OF SANDSTONE AS THE MAIN MATERIAL, IN COMBINATION WITH THE
SUBTLETY OF THE COLOUR PALETTE AND CAREFUL MANAGEMENT OF PATTERN,
TEXTURE AND DETAILING, ALLOWS PHINDA GETTY HOUSE TO STRIKE A WELL-BALANCED
DIALOGUE WITH ITS ENVIRONMENT.

Despite the supremely luxurious credentials and sophisticated atmosphere of Phinda Getty House, both its architect and interior designer – Nick Plewman and Conservation Corporation Africa's creative director Chris Browne, respectively – have demonstrated a restraint that intentionally plays down the owners' illustrious provenance and instead invites guests to play home from home while also taking in the spectacular beauty of the natural environment.

That the building's vernacular is reminiscent of a classically South African farmhouse (with its thick stone walls and thatched roof) is no mere architectural conceit – the massive sandstone blocks that constitute the spine of the structure are in fact reclaimed materials from an old rural barn that were transported to the site. For architect Plewman, the choice of these building materials was an act of appreciation for both the location's and the owners' unspoilt character. 'The walls of old sandstone anchor the structure in time as well as place,' he explains.

A linear layout was chosen to allow the homestead to snugly recline into the contours of its broadly sloped, hilly site. This arrangement of the public spaces and four private suites also acts to orient every room towards the spectacular views outside, the experience of taking in the vistas further facilitated by a façade largely comprised of floor-to-ceiling glass walls. Unstained wooden decking outdoors and light grey screed floors inside complement the simplicity of the sandstone, demonstrating the architect's preference for reducing unnecessary detail or visual distraction. An interior configuration of free-flowing spaces on different levels emphasises the design team's intention of creating a place suited to relaxed, low-key family living.

'The interior style of Phinda Getty,' affirms Chris Browne, 'is that of cool, modern Africa.' While the handcrafted leather chandeliers, custom-designed rugs, decorative fabric window panels and other statement pieces by South African textile artist Jenny Gifford provide a pleasantly flamboyant surprise, the underlying design ethos is low-key and unpretentious. Evidence of this begins with the principally neutral colour scheme, a calming palette of pale beetroot, nutmeg, washed greys and popcorn white. The interiors are further marked by a discernible absence of clutter, with the architecture providing a backdrop for the owners' collection of antiques and personal memorabilia in combination with a few select pieces of Africana and Indian artefacts. New furniture was chosen for its clean lines, comfort and resilience to both humid bush conditions and the family's boisterous young children. Suites are luxurious without being fussy, and the beds and generously proportioned baths positioned to take full advantage of the views – as is the rectangular rim-flow infinity pool, which is lined with pale grey quartz mosaic tiles and is poetically described by the architect as 'a ramp to the sky.'

The villa rate here includes your own game ranger, 4x4 excursions, butler and chef, ensuring that your every request is indulged. The point that will be emphasised most during your stay at Phinda Getty House, however, is to make yourself at home.

Jack's Camp

JACK'S CAMP

Named after the legendary big game hunter and safari operator Jack Bousfield and founded by his son Ralph together with partner Catherine Raphaely, Jack's Camp is the flagship of the couple's Uncharted Africa Safari Co and resonates with the spirit of five generations of pioneers, adventurers, hunters and conservationists. Just as remarkable as the provenance of Jack's Camp is its location – Botswana's untouched Makgadikgadi pans in the Kalahari desert. In parts of this forbiddingly dry environment the rains fall so infrequently that any paths made by man off the beaten track may last for years. And yet life in all its forms thrives here, from proud baobabs and thorny acacias to desert creatures such as aardvark, gemsbok, the elusive brown hyena and motley crews of meerkat. During the wet season certain regions of the landscape are transformed, their lush and watery grasslands luring flamingo, migratory herds of zebra and wildebeest – and the predators that hunt them.

Though replete with luxury and comfort, Jack's Camp is not a bush hotel.
In both its atmosphere and decoration it holds true to the old-fashioned glamour
of the safaris of the 1920s, reflecting a classic sense of style that is romantic,
bohemian, suffused with history and sufficiently robust to stand up to the
savage beauty of what lies beyond the tent flaps.

There are still many parallels between the rough-and-ready camp established by the late Jack Bousfield in the Makgadikgadi in the 1960s and Jack's Camp in its current incarnation as one of the world's most highly praised high-end bush destinations. The underlying notion that a tented safari should be an experience that brings one closer to the basic pleasures of the wild continues to inform all of Ralph Bousfield and Catherine Raphaely's decisions in their running of the camp. Lanterns, fires and stars are still the only sources of light when night falls. Wet kikois instead of generator-run air conditioners cool you down. Rinsing off can still be done under the heavens, though there's plenty of hot water to help take the chill off. And Jack Bousfield's legend still looms large as guests are regaled with stories of his adventures and faced with his leonine image in groupings of black-and-white photographs.

Catherine Raphaely brings her stylist's eye and unerring attention to detail into play at all of Uncharted Africa's camps and here she has crafted an authentic African colonial interior with all its inherent elegance. Campaign furniture, wooden military chests, dark hardwood four-poster beds, Persian rugs, polished brass objects and other period pieces (most of them family heirlooms, some recreated by her talented pool of artisans) lay the functional foundations for a panoply of rich colours and sumptuous textures. Red velvet, Anglo-Indian and North African textiles, ticking stripes, zebra and springbok hides, crisp cotton and cracked leather in combination with the furniture serve to imbue the tents (there are 10 in all) and public spaces with a sense of stately sophistication. Catherine Raphaely's inimitably refined touch also extends to the walls and ceilings of the canvas tents, which have been lined with a Victorian-inspired fabric wallpaper – the result of a design collaboration between herself and two of her 'very whimsical friends'.

Like his father, Ralph Bousfield is a pioneering naturalist whose interests extend beyond flora and fauna to archaeology, paleoanthropology, geology and the culture of the local Bushmen. A happy consequence of decades of hunting and gathering is that Jack's Camp is like a gigantic cabinet of curiosities: botanical, insect and wildlife drawings, photographs and etchings as well as extensive family collections of antique maps, bones and skulls, fossils, taxidermied animals, beadwork, and prehistoric tools have been curated by Catherine Raphaely and displayed in fascinating installations.

Here, tradition and eccentricity are flawlessly united in an atmosphere that really is without equal. 'As well as our position in this extraordinary natural environment, Jack's is so layered and has so many years of collections, heirlooms, bespoke pieces and items given to us by friends and guests that it would be impossible to recreate or imitate, even for me,' says Catherine. And while he was not one to concern himself with frivolous discussions of aesthetics or decoration, one can imagine Jack's gnarled countenance looking down and smiling in approval at the authentic character of this splendid camp, which continues to honour his legacy.

Singita Ebony

SINGITA EBONY

Those seeking rewarding game viewing and quiet repose find it in the tranquil setting of Singita Ebony Lodge, built in the cool shade of knobthorn and jackalberry trees on the banks of the Sand River. Time that is not spent observing the spectacular daily theatre that plays itself out on the plains of the Sabi Sand Game Reserve and commanding riverbank below is dedicated to unwinding in the lavish colonial-style atmosphere. Of all the nine Singita lodges, it is Singita Ebony that errs the most on the side of a traditional aesthetic replete with a collection of carefully curated evocative artefacts and a rich palette of jewel colours.

THOUGH INTENTIONALLY ROOTED IN THE PAST, SINGITA EBONY IS ALSO FIRMLY
CONNECTED TO THE PRESENT DUE TO A FOCUS ON CONTEMPORARY CONVENIENCES AND
A PHILOSOPHY OF MAKING GUESTS FEEL AS IF THEY HAVE ENTERED A HOME FROM HOME
— ALBEIT A DISTINCTLY GLAMOROUS AND UNDENIABLY LUXURIOUS ONE.

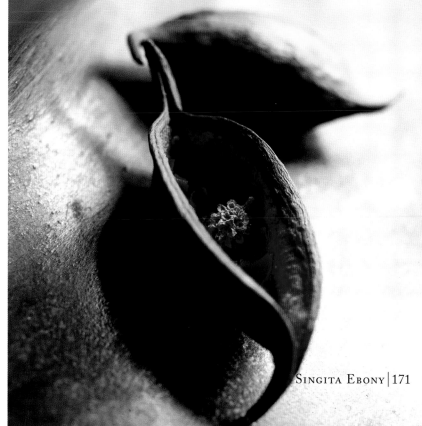

It's often said that the Singita group – under the leadership of entrepreneur Luke Bailes – can claim to have initiated the transformation of the ecotourism experience from simple communion with nature to the luxury safari experience it is today, and that this change was signalled by the opening of Ebony Lodge in 1994. Before Singita Ebony, the bush experience meant canvas cots, enamel tableware, basic cuisine and even more basic amenities. Romantic, certainly. Sumptuous, no. But with its debut came innovative ideas about decor and levels of service, and subsequently architecture, which were to revolutionise the industry.

In this instance, visitors are presented with a design that references the European colonial heritage in combination with ethnic accents that celebrate an African locality. Bruce Stafford created the robust architectural backdrop against which Boyd Ferguson and Paul van den Berg of Cécile & Boyd's have established a supremely welcoming interior, with various settings in which guests can convene or to which they may choose to retreat. Period chests, tables and bookcases, antique lighting, authentic hunting memorabilia, intricate carvings and an edited selection of Africana – some items are family heirlooms sourced from the owner's home – offset deep wing-back armchairs and gracious sofas in the atmospheric main sitting room. A highly polished floor, its layers of wax imparting a nostalgic, masculine fragrance, adds to the comforting country-house mood.

Soft furnishings are essential to expressing the overall design concept, one that merges tradition with the rich cultural heritage of Africa. So gently worn needlepoint and chintz-covered scatter cushions highlight the unique patterns and textured qualities of kente cloths and kikois; linen on the outdoor dining tables is made of custom-designed fabric handpainted with southern African flora and sewn to resemble Xhosa skirts with their distinctive layers; and, in the central lounge, four Masai Mara-red painted columns have been draped with kilims lined with raw silk.

One of the unifying elements of the decor at Singita Ebony Lodge is its opulent palette of energetic reds, oranges and yellows – inspired by beaded tribal jewellery and made even more dazzling by a background of archetypal colonial shades from mahogany to russet to tan.

Away from the public areas, the interiors of the 12 villas – each with outdoor shower and private plunge pool – are equally well-groomed. Though deliberately pared down in comparison with the public spaces, colonial-style flourishes do make an appearance in the suites. Examples include the warthog-tusk handles on wardrobes in the dressing rooms and canopied mahogany beds covered in berry-red throws. A signature of all the Singita lodges is their well-appointed bathrooms, and those at Ebony do not disappoint. Black slate floors, an antique-style bath, his-and-hers chocolate-coloured vanities and glass-enclosed shower make the bathroom into an attractive extension of the living area.

It is the combination of faded colonial grandeur with vibrant colour and intricate detailing that is the key to Singita Ebony's enduring charm, an appeal that has secured it a place in safari lore as both an industry pioneer and a modern classic.

SANDIBE SAFARI LODGE

Sandibe

For visitors to Sandibe Safari Lodge in Botswana, the experience begins while flying over semi-arid savannah grasslands that gradually morph into the emerald-green patchwork that is the Okavango delta from the air. This inland river delta – the biggest in the world – is referred to in ancient tradition as the river that never finds the sea and its lagoons, islands and channels form the habitat of a vast array of animals and plant life on a slowly meandering path that ends in the Kalahari desert. Sandibe, located on a permanent channel in the delta overlooking the Santantadibe river, is adjacent to the world-famous Moremi Game Reserve and functions as a thoughtfully conceived man-made habitat for the two-legged species that come to observe the natural splendour of this fertile wetland wilderness.

Sandibe's earthy design communicates an easy relationship with nature, blending effortlessly with the thick reed beds and towering trees of the immediate surroundings while also providing for three of the most important luxury safari requirements: privacy, security and comfort.

The Botswanan government's strict environmental and tourism policies have ensured that the Okavango delta is one of Africa's last great unspoilt wildernesses, and a similarly ethical and ecosensitive approach also forms the underlying design concept of Sandibe Safari Lodge. Like all of architect Nick Plewman's work for Conservation Corporation Africa, this lodge exhibits an instinctive response to the site with its riparian location and thick belt of forest fringe. Sandibe has been built with a commitment to 'treading lightly on the earth,' says Plewman, and its organic architecture evokes the living forest. 'No trees were sacrificed in the building of the lodge,' he explains. 'Instead, the eight cottages were built in a natural clearing.' Furthermore, any saplings that needed removing were carefully transplanted into the surrounding forest.

While the aesthetic directives called for in the original brief from client are evident in the traditional adobe-style, thick mud walls (bringing to mind the giant termite hills that are such an intrinsic part of the scenery) and subtle pan-African references (such as the rondavels, or round private cottages), the architect garnered much of his inspiration by living on the site for several months before construction began. For hundreds of years herds of elephant have walked the paths that run through Sandibe, a phenomenon witnessed by the architect and one that provided further motivation for the design team not to alter the face of the landscape in any way. All the building materials, including thatch and wood (which have a natural tendency to weather and thus blend into the environs) as well as large swathes of glass were chosen to harmonise with nature and set the buildings within the surrounding vegetation, not on top of it. The resulting transition between indoors and out is one that is absolutely seamless.

Guest areas are for the most part open to the elements and are defined by levels: a top-floor library, ground-floor dining room and generously proportioned, sunken sitting room, all tucked beneath a soaring canopy of trees. Shaded decks slung with hammocks afford views across the peaceful waterway and to the grasslands beyond.

The interior style of Sandibe is described by Conservation Corporation Africa's design custodian Chris Browne as 'Organic Delta', his starting point for the decor inspired by the large marquesia-tree columns that support the roof of the main guest areas. The burnished copper colour of their bark has taken root on decorative items such as oversized hanging lanterns, picture frames and ethnic anklets as well as soft furnishings, including the copper-coloured mosquito nets that feature so prominently in each cottage. While the additional earthy tones of chocolate, toffee and clay affirm the rustic nature of Sandibe, it is these glints of copper that serve to inject a sense of glamour and subtle shine.

More evidence of the organic influence is apparent in the thick, woven textures on flat surfaces, a handful of carvings and the appealing handcrafted imperfection of Botswana basketware and gently worn leather bedspreads. Just as the Okavango river is in no hurry to get to its final destination, visitors to this particular part of the delta are reluctant to leave this watery wonderland and the warm, welcoming oasis that is Sandibe Safari Lodge.

Wolwedans

To describe the locations of the several camps that make up the Wolwedans Collection of lodges as 'remote' might come across as the ultimate understatement; after all, they are situated in Namibia's vast desert environment. But even deserts can become too overcrowded for those seeking true solitude. The NamibRand Nature Reserve is a place of utter seclusion thanks to it being largely overlooked by the tour buses and self-drive 4x4 crowds who instead opt to visit its better-known and somewhat more accessible counterpart, Sossusvlei. This is a virtually untouched part of the world that comprises several habitats, from the shrubby desert grasslands and surging red dune belts to rocky mountain outcrops tinged violet by the setting sun. Wolwedans Dunes Lodge and Wolwedans Private Camp find themselves in the midst of all this serenity, ably fulfilling their function as welcoming shelters that stand in deference to the austere beauty of the landscape.

WOLWEDANS DUNES LODGE, PERCHED ON TOP OF A DUNE PLATEAU, AND WOLWEDANS PRIVATE CAMP, SET IN THE HUSHED SECLUSION OF A VALLEY, HAVE BOTH BEEN GUIDED BY THE AESTHETIC PRINCIPLES OF SIMPLICITY, UTILITARIANISM AND UNPARALLELED CONTACT WITH THE ELEMENTS.

In creating Wolwedans Dunes Lodge and Wolwedans Private Camp, Stephan Brueckner (who is the owner, chief designer and managing director of the Wolwedans Collection portfolio) has created two equally appealing destinations that engage in an active dialogue with their settings. Wolwedans Private Camp is the more intimate of the two, a self-contained stand-alone 'suite' accommodating no more than four guests and comprising two bedrooms, two bathrooms, indoor and outdoor living rooms and an open-plan kitchen. The building takes the shape of a low-slung cabin and is constructed of wood, a corrugated-iron roof and canvas sheets that replace fixed windows and roll up to reveal the straw-coloured grass plains outside. Decor is classically inclined: deep leather couches, warm colours, paraffin lanterns and collectibles redolent with history evoke a home-from-home atmosphere.

The emphasis here is on relaxation and privacy. Browsing the well-stocked library, taking solitary walks on the plains, luxuriating in afternoon naps on the shaded veranda and enjoying the languorous preparation of one's own meals (all food and beverages are supplied) are the stress-free activities that occupy those who choose to include Private Camp on their Wolwedans agenda. Visitors from more pampered backgrounds have the option of requesting the services of a private chef and personal field guide, should the thought of going it alone prove too daunting. Wolwedans Dunes Lodge corresponds to Wolwedans Private Camp in its use of the same fundamentally simple materials and clean-lined architecture. The nine wooden guest chalets are set comfortably apart from each other on the dunes and have been slightly elevated off the ground on stilts. Canvas blinds take the place of windows and allow the space to be opened to the elements in every direction bar the western side, which is made of solid wood in order to protect the chalets' inhabitants from the prevailing winds. 'The idea,' says Brueckner, 'was not to attract attention to the buildings. The structures are deliberately not generic in appearance nor are they reminiscent of a particular vernacular.' The decoration of the suites is stylish and comfortable but underpinned by an element of careful restraint that allows the views, and not the trimmings, to play hero. 'We've kept the bedrooms very simple,' explains Brueckner. 'There are only natural, subdued colours and no paintings or photographs on the walls. Once you open those canvas blinds, well, that's the best picture you could ever wish to see.' One of the lodge's most dramatic spaces is the Mountain View Suite, a pagoda-like structure set away from the main camp and exposed to nature on all sides.

The architectural simplicity of the chalets is continued in the main complex, which consists of an inviting series of lounges, sun decks, pool, communal fireplace, tea deck, library, wine cellar and two dining rooms. The decor here is slightly more layered and colourful than in the private areas and reflects a colonial-chic sensibility. A palette of ochre and sand forms the ideal backdrop to traditional and unpretentious pieces: deep leather sofas, dark wood furniture, a handsome collection of antiques and the lodge's signature paraffin lamps, which allow the stars in the night sky to garner their due attention.

LION SANDS IVORY LODGE

Ivory Lodge

Gently nestled on the lush banks of the Sabie river, in the vast southern portion of the Sabi Sand Game Reserve that borders the Kruger National Park, Lion Sands Ivory Lodge is perfectly positioned to take in the endless procession of animals that arrives to slake their thirst at the water's edge, as well as the magnificent predators who come to hunt them. The low-slung structure – consisting of six suites set around a communal lodge and linked by raised walkways – seeks to embrace the lay of the land with an environmentally mindful design that revolves entirely around the lodge's river-facing aspect.

BOTH THE ARCHITECTURAL AND INTERIOR-DESIGN LANGUAGE HERE SPEAK OF BALANCE:

A PLEASING ACCORD BETWEEN TRADITION AND MODERNITY, EBONY AND IVORY,

SOLIDITY AND LIGHTNESS, SIMPLICITY AND SOPHISTICATION.

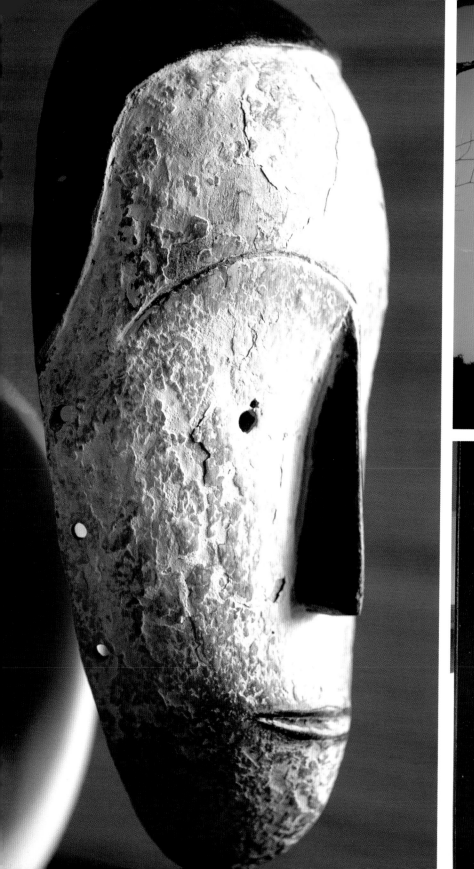

In designing Lion Sands Ivory Lodge, architects Paul and Karen Wygers of Urban Solutions have expertly realised their objective of creating a building that blends into the context of its surroundings, 'allowing the powerful quiet and solitude of the bush, not the structure, to dominate.'

The architecture is also remarkable in its amalgamation of the traditional with the new. The thatch, for example, a very familiar building material, has been used for the roofs of the self-contained suites. However, in this contemporary update it takes the form of a modern gabled structure that, in the bedrooms, has been inset with a large sheet of glass for floor-to-ceiling drama. Apart from the obvious intention of framing the vista outside, these enormous windows mean that by day the rooms are illuminated by natural light, while at night a canopy of stars comes into view.

The traditional notion of the safari-lodge suite has also been revisited, allowing guests more flexibility in how they experience the spaces. Units are accessed via a meandering path that breaks away from a raised timber public walkway. Each unit itself consists of three interconnected areas: a central courtyard with infinity pool flanked on either side by an *en suite* bedroom and living room. Once behind the large carved mahogany doors to their unit, guests can choose how to spend their time: game viewing from the cool of the plunge pool, reclining on the canopied bed, soaking in the organically shaped bath or colonising the comfortable living room with its large fireplace, clean-lined furniture and ebony-and-ivory colour scheme.

According to the architects, the design process was not without its challenges. Removing any plant life was not an option, so the entire structure including the communal areas (incorporating a boma, restaurant, viewing decks, bar, lounge, spa and library) was manipulated around the existing rocky outcrops and trees.

The job of refurbishing the lodge was recently undertaken by interior designer Paula Hattingh, who has created a classic contemporary feel that is made warm and engaging via the use of texture and the addition of a number of carefully chosen African objets such as Bamileke stools, horn bowls, inlaid boxes and carved headrests. The neutral colour scheme of off-whites anchored by chic black is very much in keeping with the associations evoked by the name 'Ivory Lodge'. An aesthetic highlight is the dried indigenous tree in the dining room, a graphic allusion to the fragile ecosystem outside.

Nowhere is the sense of a borderless space more apparent than in the lodge's two tree-house escapes, which offer guests a unique overnight experience. Here the furnishings are luxurious but simple (a generously proportioned four-poster bed with mosquito net, plus canvas director's chairs, a bush table and antique wooden vanity with double basins) ensuring that the focus is directed where it should be – on the glorious natural elements above, below and around you.

directory

ALL TRAVEL FACILITATED BY FRASER'S AFRICAN DESTINATIONS
T: +27 (0) 21 426 5808   F: +27 (0) 21 487 6859   C: +27 (0) 82 378 6632
E: angus@tourismcapetown.co.za   www.frasersad.co.za

EXETER LEADWOOD LODGE
Location: Sabi Sand Game Reserve, Kruger National Park, South Africa
T: +27 (0) 11 809 4300   F: +27 (0) 11 809 4400
E: reservations@ccafrica.com   www.ccafrica.com
Architect: Nick Plewman   T: +27 (0) 11 482 7133
E: nick@plewmanarchitects.co.za
Interior designer: Câline Williams-Wynn   T: +27 (0) 82 600 7546
E: caline@arti.co.za

HUNTER'S MARATABA
Location: Marakele National Park, Limpopo, South Africa
T: +27 (0) 44 532 7818   F: +27 (0) 44 501 1100
E: res@hunterhotels.com   www.hunterhotels.com
Architect: Nick Plewman   T: +27 (0) 11 482 7133
E: nick@plewmanarchitects.co.za
Interior designers: Jill and Jacqui Hunter   T: +27 (0) 21 423 7870
E: jacqui.hunter@telkomsa.net

JACK'S CAMP
Location: Makgadikgadi-Nxai Pans National Park, Botswana
T: +27 (0) 11 447 1605   F: +27 (0) 11 447 6905
E: reservations@unchartedafrica.com   www.unchartedafrica.com
Designer: Catherine Raphaely   T: +27 (0) 11 447 1605
E: reservations@unchartedafrica.com

LION SANDS IVORY LODGE
Location: Sabi Sand Game Reserve, Kruger National Park, South Africa
T: +27 (0) 11 484 9911   F: +27 (0) 11 484 9916
E: res@lionsands.com   www.lionsands.com
Architects: Paul and Karen Wygers Urban Solutions
T: +27 (0) 11 833 7622   E: karen@urbansolutions.co.za
Interior designer: Paula Hattingh   T: +27 (0) 82 966 3588
E: paulahattingh@telkomsa.net

LITTLE KULALA
Location: Kulala Wilderness Reserve, Sossusvlei, Namibia
T: +27 (0) 11 807 1800   F: +27 (0) 11 807 2110
E: enquiry@wilderness.co.za   www.wilderness-safaris.com
Architect: Andy Chase
Interior designer: Laurie Owen   T: +27 (0) 83 636 8887 +27 (0) 83 636 8880
E: laurieointeriors@telkomsa.net

MADIKWE SAFARI LODGE
Location: Madikwe Game Reserve, North West Province, South Africa
T: +27 (0) 11 809 4300   F: +27 (0) 11 809 4400
E: reservations@ccafrica.com   www.ccafrica.com
Architect: Rob Marnewick   T: +27 (0) 82 466 3871 +27 (0) 12 349 2437
Interior designer: Chris Browne   T: +27 (0) 11 809 4300
E: information@ccafrica.com

NGALA TENTED CAMP
Location: Ngala Private Game Reserve, Kruger National Park, South Africa
T: +27 (0) 11 809 4300   F: +27 (0) 11 809 4400
E: reservations@ccafrica.com   www.ccafrica.com
Architect: Nick Plewman   T: +27 (0) 11 482 7133
E: nick@plewmanarchitects.co.za
Interior designer: Chris Browne   T: +27 (0) 11 809 4300
E: information@ccafrica.com

THE OUTPOST
Location: Kruger National Park, South Africa
T: +27 (0) 11 245 5700   F: +27 (0) 11 884 9063
E: dee@klpg.co.za   www.theoutpost.co.za
Architect: Enrico Daffonchio   T: +27 (0) 11 447 8118   E: sadac@iafrica.com
Interior designers: Christoff van Staden and Peter Aucamp
T: + 27 (0) 11 341 0282   E: info@mix.co.za

PHINDA GETTY HOUSE
Location: Phinda Private Game Reserve, KwaZulu-Natal, South Africa
T: +27 (0) 11 809 4300   F: +27 (0) 11 809 4400
E: reservations@ccafrica.com   www.ccafrica.com
Architect: Nick Plewman   T: +27 (0) 11 482 7133
E: nick@plewmanarchitects.co.za
Interior designer: Chris Browne   T: +27 (0) 11 809 4300
E: information@ccafrica.com

Planet Baobab
Location: Gweta, Makgadikgadi Salt Pans, Botswana
T: +27 (0) 11 447 1605   F: +27 (0) 11 447 6905
E: reservations@unchartedafrica.com   www.unchartedafrica.com
Designer: Catherine Raphaely   T: +27 (0) 11 447 1605
E: reservations@unchartedafrica.com

Sandibe Safari Lodge
Location: Moremi Game Reserve, Botswana
T: +27 (0) 11 809 4300   F: +27 (0) 11 809 4400
E: reservations@ccafrica.com   www.ccafrica.com
Architect: Nick Plewman   T: +27 (0) 11 482 7133
E: nick@plewmanarchitects.co.za
Interior designer: Chris Browne   T: +27 (0) 11 809 4300
E: information@ccafrica.com

Singita Boulders
Location: Singita Private Game Reserve, South Africa
T: +27 (0) 21 683 3424   F: +27 (0) 21 671 6776
E: singita@singita.co.za   www.singita.com
Architect: Bruce Stafford (Sydney, Australia)   T: +61 (02) 9327 7889
E: info@brucestafford.com
Interior designers: Cécile & Boyd's   T: +27 (0) 21 425 5110
E: design@cecileandboyd.co.za

Singita Ebony
Location: Sabi Sand Game Reserve, Kruger National Park, South Africa
T: +27 (0) 21 683 3424   F: +27 (0) 21 671 6776
E: singita@singita.co.za   www.singita.com
Architect: Bruce Stafford (Sydney, Australia)   T: +61 (02) 9327 7889
E: info@brucestafford.com
Interior designers: Cécile & Boyd's   T: +27 (0) 21 425 5110
E: design@cecileandboyd.co.za

Singita Lebombo
Location: Kruger National Park, South Africa
T: +27 (0) 21 683 3424   F: +27 (0) 21 671 6776
E: singita@singita.co.za   www.singita.com
Architects: Andrew Makin and Janina Masojada
OMM Design Workshop   T: +27 (0) 31 303 5191
E: janina@designworkshop.co.za
Joy Brasler   T: +27 (0) 31 208 7810   E: joy@davice.co.za
Interior designers: Cécile & Boyd's   T: +27 (0) 21 425 5110
E: design@cecileandboyd.co.za

Singita Sweni
Location: Kruger National Park, South Africa
T: +27 (0) 21 683 3424   F: +27 (0) 21 671 6776
E: singita@singita.co.za   www.singita.com
Architects: Andrew Makin and Janina Masojada
OMM Design Workshop   T: +27 (0) 31 303 5191
E: janina@designworkshop.co.za
Joy Brasler   T: +27 (0) 31 208 7810   E: joy@davice.co.za
Interior designers: Cécile & Boyd's   T: +27 (0) 21 425 5110
E: design@cecileandboyd.co.za

Vumbura Plains Camp
Location: Okavango Delta, Botswana
T: +27 (0) 11 807 1800   F: +27 (0) 11 807 2110
E: enquiry@wilderness.co.za   www.wilderness-safaris.com
Architects and interior designers: Silvio Rech and Lesley Carstens
T: +27 (0) 486 1525 +27 (0) 82 900 9935
E: adventarch@mweb.co.za
Interior designers: George Boorsma and Lisebo Mokhesi
T: + 27 (0) 11 784 0704   E: george@inkdesignlab.co.za

Wolwedans Dunes & Wolwedans Private Camp
Location: NamibRand Nature Reserve, Namibia
T: +26 4 61 230 616   +26 4 61 220 102
E: reservations@wolwedans.com.na   www.wolwedans.com
Designer: Stephan Brueckner

acknowledgements

Thank you to all the lodges and their staff for the hospitality and enthusiasm for this project. Thanks also to all the designers, architects and decorators for redefining the term Safari Style. You made this book an exciting journey where we marvelled at your creativity and originality every step of the way.

– Craig Fraser and Libby Doyle

**QUIVERTREE
PUBLICATIONS**

PHOTOGRAPHS CRAIG FRASER ❙ **WORDS** MANDY ALLEN
COPY EDITOR ROBYN ALEXANDER ❙ **DESIGN & PRODUCTION** LIBBY DOYLE

This edition is the second printing of THE NEW SAFARI:DESIGN/DECOR/DETAIL

FIRST PUBLISHED IN 2007 BY QUIVERTREE PUBLICATIONS
PO Box 51051 • Waterfront • 8002 • Cape Town • South Africa
T: +27 (0) 21 461 6808 • **F:** +27 (0) 21 461 6842 • **E:** info@quivertree.co.za
www.quivertree.co.za

DISTRIBUTED BY QUIVERTREE PUBLICATIONS
PO Box 51051 • Waterfront • 8002 • Cape Town • South Africa
T: +27 (0) 21 461 6808 • **F:** +27 (0) 21 461 6842 • **E:** info@quivertree.co.za

ISBN: 978-0-9802651-0-1

QUIVERTREE
PUBLICATIONS

THE BATHROOM

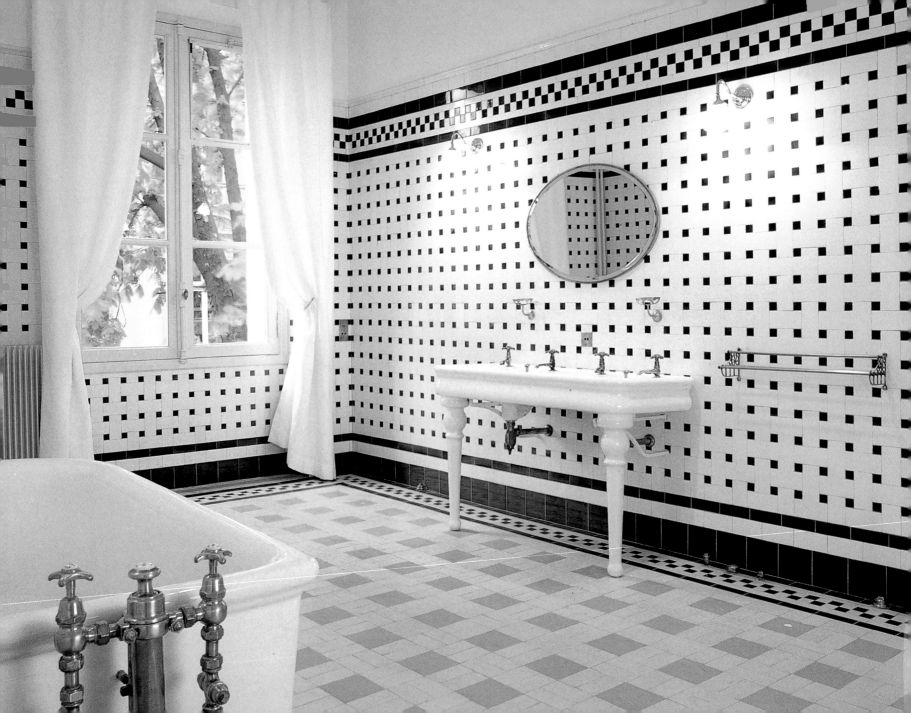

Diane Berger

THE BATHROOM

Photographs by Fritz von der Schulenburg

Abbeville Press ❧ Publishers ❧ New York ❧ London ❧ Paris

DEDICATION

To my husband, Tom, who happily shared my pipe dream of a bathroom harking back to another era, faces life without a power shower, and is so far delighted to continue the tradition in Provence.

"Luxury must be comfortable, otherwise it is not luxury," Coco Chanel once said, perhaps unaware that she was describing exactly what the perfect bathroom should be. This book is dedicated to helping you find your personal bath style and marry your own definition of luxury to your own sense of comfort, whether pared-down basics or yards of marble.

JACKET FRONT: This warm, handsomely appointed bathroom was designed by Christophe Gollut (see also page 113).

JACKET BACK: Colored images of wildlife add a touch of the outdoors to this inviting bathroom designed by Antony Little (see also page 80).

FRONTISPIECE: In a Parisian apartment, a spacious, 1930s-style bathroom demonstrates the form-follows-function approach to bathroom design: the inherently ornamental effect of geometric tiles is supported by a few basic elements, including a curvaceous period tub, an old-fashioned radiator, and a double-pedestal sink.

PAGES 6 AND 7: The bathroom of the late Duke of Windsor features a specially designed cabinet and a lacquer-backed grooming set.

EDITOR: Jacqueline Decter
MANUSCRIPT EDITOR: Todd Lyon
DESIGNER: Molly Shields
PRODUCTION EDITOR: Abigail Asher
PRODUCTION MANAGER: Lou Bilka

First edition
10 9 8 7 6 5 4 3 2 1

Additional photography credits
Courtesy of Al Fayed Archives/Fritz von der Schulenburg: pp. 6, 7, 126, 127.
© 1990 Archivi Alinari/Art Resource, New York: p. 9.
© The Board of Trustees of the Victoria & Albert Museum: p. 11.
British Architectural Library, RIBA, London/A.C. Cooper Ltd., London: p. 12. © Sibyl Colefax and John Fowler/Michael Dunne: p. 81.
The Interior Archive Ltd/Simon Brown: p. 26 right; Tim Clinch: pp. 26 left, 27; James Mortimer: p. 58; Christopher Simon Sykes: p. 135; Henry Wilson: pp. 88, 122.

Library of Congress Cataloging-in-Publication Data
Berger, Diane (Diane L.)
    The bathroom / Diane Berger ; photographs by Fritz von der Schulenburg.
      p. cm.
    Includes bibliographical references and index.
    ISBN 0-7892-0086-4
    1. Bathrooms. 2. Interior decoration. I. Von der Schulenburg, Fritz. II. Title.
NK2117.B33B47   1996
747.7'8—dc20   96-12130

CONTENTS

INTRODUCTION

It is the place of blissful escape where we steal a few moments of precious privacy. It is the place to which we flee to make ourselves feel good—to relax, rejuvenate, recharge. Its importance goes well beyond the mundane practical functions of personal maintenance and the rituals of hygiene; it is where we cleanse ourselves spiritually as well as physically.

During various periods in its colorful history, the bathroom has enjoyed an elevated status in the home. Until the late nineteenth or early twentieth century, bathrooms were extravagances reserved for the rich, and that halo of luxury still exists today. Though small in size, it is the room in which we find some of our greatest personal pleasures—and its decorative potential is enormous.

Bathroom design and decoration are rooted in a hierarchy of need fulfillment that begins with the functional and moves to the emotional and psychological. Every good bathroom is built around a kit of fittings and fixtures. Choosing these basics is a question of "bath style"—are you someone who loves a long soak, or would you rather have a speedy shower?—but once those simple preferences have been determined, it

is the nuances of private pleasures that guide your design decisions. With a dizzying array of decorating options, ranging from the look of a rustic farmhouse to the gilded splendor of an imperial palace, it helps to narrow the field by determining your personal "feel-good" factor.

Ask yourself: How do you want to feel when you're in your ultimate bathroom? What would you most like to gaze at from the tub? Do you want your bathroom to be as comfortable as a sitting room, with all the trappings of a proper parlor, or do you prefer gleaming expanses of squeaky-clean tile? When you begin to imagine ideal environments, you'll find that the bathroom serves a multitude of functions, both emotional and physical, on a daily basis. In the morning, we may race to it to psych ourselves up to face the world. Under the pulse of a shower or in the depths of a hot bath we might strategize, compose, and energize ourselves to meet the demands of the day. It is in the bathroom that we revert to our most natural state—nudity—but we also construct artifice, fashioning our outward selves for public presentation. In the midst of our nonprivate lives, we slip into the bathroom at various times of the day to have a moment alone, to look into the mirror and remind ourselves of who we are. At nightfall the bathroom is our restorative haven, the place where we literally let our hair down. There we can spend quiet time regrouping and editing, reconstructing our remembered day into something to save. Throughout any given week we retreat to the bathroom in the pursuit of luxury, therapy, healing, pampering, intimacy, solace, beauty. It is a place of self-transformation, where our outermost and innermost selves converge.

For all these reasons, the bathroom is a special place. Naturally we want it to look special, and the fulfillment of that wish requires energy, introspection, imagination, and an understanding of our own needs and desires. Of these, imagination is perhaps the most important—thinking about a place you may have taken for granted and seeing it in a new way. Do you want to start the day with a muscle-pounding power shower? Do you long to lounge in a tub filled with essential oils, immersed in the pages of a steamy novel? Whether you yearn for the sparkle of high-tech chic (pages 124 and 125) or the ambience of an Edwardian gentleman's dressing room (page 115), you can make a splash and transform even the most ordinary space into a real bathing beauty.

The modern bathroom has come a long way since its earliest manifestations—and the refinement of personal cleanliness is only one small part of the picture. The room we consider private to the point of sanctity had, at various times during its evolution, a very public image. It has been a status symbol, a center of social life, and has even played a part in courtship rituals, celebrations, and entertainment.

For the ancients, bathing was a public affair where ritual reigned supreme. Private baths did exist in ancient Greece—one notable example was the Queen's bathroom in the Palace of Knossos at Crete (ca. 2000 B.C.), which was whimsically decorated with water motifs—but for most Greeks, bathing was a communal activity. The baths were a meeting ground where gossip was shared, politics were discussed, contacts were made, and business was informally conducted.

In ancient Rome, the social significance of the public bath reached an apotheosis. Roman baths were architecturally impressive and opulently decorated, often consisting of a collection of rooms ritualistically arranged within elegant garden complexes. Bathing was not a do-it-yourself operation: servants would pour water over the bathers from a series of containers and anoint them with oils. The bath's association with wealth no doubt had its roots in antiquity. The sheer laboriousness of the process and the key role of servants earned it a reputation as a luxurious leisure activity, even though both rich and poor visited the baths in ancient times. As for private baths, these, too were found in elite Roman villas, but they did not diminish the importance of public bathing and its association with both sensual pleasure and social status.

After the Roman Empire's demise, the nature of bathing, along with the whole of domestic life, changed profoundly. By the Norman period, domestic architecture had taken on a communal character. Individual rooms were not assigned to specific functions; daily activities were centered in a cavernous hall. Privacy was an alien concept in these heavily populated settings. There, family members, retainers, employees, and guests would eat, cook, sleep, socialize, and even raise animals. When bathing was desired, large, round wooden tubs were brought to the hall and filled with heated water poured from jugs.

During the Middle Ages, a number of monasteries featured rooms with multiple tubs. There were conflicting attitudes toward the use of them, however. Some monks regarded washing as an act of piety, while others felt it was more religiously correct not to bathe. Among the general population there was a belief that water spread disease, and these concerns surrounded monastic baths as well as public baths. In the private arena, however, it appears that some people were more concerned with status than with piety when it came to washing. Illuminated manuscripts and paintings of the Middle Ages and Renaissance (see illustration on this page) depict bathing as an important part of upper-class social life. Wooden tubs, designed to seat at least two people, were lined with linens

—a potent sign of wealth due to their rarity and expense. These liners, often edged with delicate embroidery, were used to shield bathers from soggy wood and/or splinters, but were also very much on display. Some tubs were even piled with pillows, which, naturally, soon became sopping wet. In other cases, tubs were topped with billowing canopies, and although their stated function was to capture steam from the bath, more likely they served the same role as the canopies that towered over beds and chairs—to confer status on their owners and literally crown them with a halo of wealth. Since many medieval landowners traveled according to planting seasons, linens were a practical way to flaunt affluence; they could be packed and unpacked as the household relocated.

Eventually, the elite act of "private" bathing was integrated into ceremonies, celebrations, and courtship rituals. Nudity, it should be noted, did not have the same associations with intimacy that it does today. So, with linens prominently in view, bathers would be wined, dined, and feted with music, and the bath became firmly established as something much more than an opportunity to become clean.

SCENE OF CONJUGAL BATHING, IN NICOLA DI SEGNA, *THE JOYS OF MARRIED LIFE.*
MUSEO CIVICO, SAN GIMIGNANO, ITALY.

9

During the Renaissance, those people fortunate enough to have bedrooms often bathed there, too. The tubs they summoned had lids that partially covered the tops to keep the steam from escaping. In posh homes, tented baths were constructed in rooms of their own. These bathrooms, although rarely found before the seventeenth century, could be extravagantly decorated. A "bathing room" at Windsor Castle was described in 1598 as "wainscoted with a looking glass." According to historian Lawrence Wright, this may have been the place where Queen Elizabeth I took her monthly bath, "whether she needed it or no." A general distrust of water continued to abound, however, keeping many people bath-free. This growing paranoia about water, combined with an increased awareness of outward appearance, gave rise to a trend of washing only the exposed parts of one's body—that is, the face and hands. Frequent changes of clothing and the power of fragrances or floral pomanders were relied upon to take care of the rest.

Turkish-style public baths witnessed a revival in seventeenth-century Europe. The original Turkish bath, popular since the Ottoman Empire, had evolved as a part of Islamic culture. It featured a progression of increasingly warm rooms through which bathers passed until they reached a steam room so hot that it was necessary to wear protective shoes. This was followed by a cool-down period in a more temperate chamber, after which bathers were treated to a rigorous massage and a fragrant wash-down. European baths borrowed some architectural forms and also adopted certain rituals from the traditional Turkish bath. One notable exception was that in a true Turkish bath women and men were strictly forbidden to mingle within its chambers. Heat, however, was still a key attraction. According to the *London Spy* in 1699, Britain's version of the Turkish bath featured water as "hot as a pastry cook's oven." Public baths, in spite of their popularity, were still viewed with suspicion by a certain portion of the population. Pepys, the seventeenth-century diarist, observed the comings and goings of one communal bather: "My wife busy in going with her woman to the hot house to bathe herself, after her long being within doors in the dirt, so that she now pretends to a resolution of being hereafter very clean. How long it will hold, I can guess. . . . me thinks it cannot be clean to go so many bodies with the same water."

While "so many bodies" shared water at the public baths, private bathrooms were becoming "showstoppers." They were still reserved for an elite few, however. Historian Peter Thornton notes that in the seventeenth century French architect Louis Savot believed bathrooms were not "necessities" but that a "grandee might want to have a bath for some other reason."

By the early eighteenth century the private bathroom was well-established as a status symbol, and important enough to figure in architectural designs. The French architect Jacques-François Blondel published a grand design for a *salle de bain* in 1738, with a matched pair of specially designed "before and after" tubs—one for washing and one for rinsing—both topped by elaborate, fabric-draped canopies (page 11). This opulent style was hardly wasted on bathers alone, however. The stylish practice of receiving visitors in one's private apartments—derived from the royal levée—put bathrooms on display for select guests. On the coveted house-tour routes of the day, visitors who ranked highly enough were able to gain access to an elite homeowner's inner chambers, including the bedroom and the bath. In 1802 English diarist and essayist Mary Berry's trip to Paris was made complete by a glimpse of Madame Récamier's ultra-chic bathroom: "Out of [her bedroom] is a beautiful little salle de bain. The walls are inlaid with satin-wood and mahogany, and slight arabesques patterns in black upon the satin-wood. The bath presents itself as a sofa in a recess, covered with a cushion of scarlet cloth embroidered and laced in black" (page 12).

The "private" bathroom, worthy of being put on display in its finery, had arrived. It was at last, in author Witold Rybczynski's words, a "fashionable accessory."

While the design of personal bathing chambers continued to evolve, certain public baths became stylish destinations. In Bath, England, for example, where the waters were believed to have therapeutic powers, the great and the good came together for the spa experience. These natural baths became the center of an elaborate social scene, including teas, dances, and assemblies. Intriguingly, it was one of the few places where the classes mixed and mingled.

In the midst of this public bath revival, private bathrooms were being outfitted with coy new accessories. Bathtubs, often copper, might be concealed in decorative rattan surrounds with high backs designed to look like sofas or daybeds, or painted with lavish decoration. These, along with chamber-pot cupboards that were often disguised as chairs, graced the pages of pattern books, such as Chippendale's, Sheraton's, and Hepplewhite's, and were treated as grandly as any other piece of household furniture.

By mid-nineteenth century the Victorian passion for creating objects to suit every need and fancy was enthusiastically directed at the bathroom. The Great Exhibition of 1851, held at the Crystal Palace in London, featured all manner of baths, including shower, traveling, sponge, slipper, and soap baths, as well as other furnishings, such as washstands and shaving stands. These were all available from manufacturers' catalogs. Prescriptive literature extolled the virtues and vices, both medical and spiritual, of various water temperatures and

DESIGN FOR A BATHROOM AND LAVATORY, c. 1738.
VICTORIA & ALBERT MUSEUM, LONDON.

11

degrees of wetness. Most enduring, however, were the advances in plumbing and manufacturing that made hot-and-cold running water available to a larger public. Servants and water carriers, though they still existed, were no longer essential to a good, hot bath, and bathroom rituals became more private. Eventually, tubs and shower baths were established as standard fixtures, and were shuttered away behind closed doors. The bathroom became the private inner sanctum we know today.

The first sinks were associated with dining and/or religious rituals. In the medieval period, hand-washing practices were strictly governed by rules laid out in etiquette manuals and prescriptive literature. At elite banquets, a servant would bring to the table a ewer or jug, often made of precious metals and ornamented with decorative motifs or the owner's coat of arms, and, in order of rank, would pour scented water over diners' outstretched hands. A basin was used to catch the overflow.

Pitchers and washbasins have since enjoyed a long history. During the Renaissance they were placed in sleeping chambers—where such chambers existed—and by the eighteenth century porcelain basins and pitchers were standard bedroom fixtures. People tended to use these for washing the "public" parts of their bodies—that is, face and hands. As the bathroom gained in status in the eighteenth century, major cabinet-makers introduced use-specific furniture, such as washstands and shaving stands, which could be placed either in the bedroom or the bathroom. The basic design of these pieces consisted of a porcelain bowl sunk neatly into a piece of decorative case furniture. With its function thus concealed, the cabinet would look appropriate in any room of the house. As the style evolved, washstands were embellished with elaborate folding tops, sometimes fitted with mirrors. Though diminutive, these cabinets were clearly status symbols.

In the nineteenth century, size mattered—at least where domestic objects were concerned. First, sinks were encased in majestic, oversized dressing tables; later, elaborate tiled back splashes were added to the

ROBERT SMIRKE, *MADAME RÉCAMIER'S BATHROOM*, 1802, COLORED DRAWING. ROYAL INSTITUTE OF BRITISH ARCHITECTS, LONDON.

12

tables to protect walls from water damage. By the late nineteenth century advances in plumbing and porcelain production gave rise to the pedestal sink, a design that endures to this day. Although running water at the turn of the tap had become available to a broad population, bowls and pitchers were still used into the twentieth century. Ironically, these could long be found in grand English country houses, because the cost of fully plumbing very large residences was prohibitive. Nevertheless, the availability of running water in private homes and the establishment of the sink as a standard fixture marked a key point in the evolution of domestic life. The water carrier, though forever fixed in the heavens, had been replaced.

Like tubs and sinks, toilets were originally portable. Although Sir John Harington, godson of Queen Elizabeth I, invented a flushing toilet in 1596, and Alexander Cummings patented his "valve closet" in England in 1775, various forms of flushing toilets remained luxuries until well into the nineteenth century. Most people used chamber pots. Historical folklore suggests that the term *loo* originated in eighteenth-century Edinburgh, when passers-by would hear a call of "Gardy-loo" (the local rendition of the French *gardez l'eau*) and know that the contents of a chamber pot were about to be flung out of a nearby window. Other historians speculate that the term may be a reference to the French usage of *petits lieux* or *lieux à l'anglaise* in architectural plans.

Early chamber pots, or "close stools," were cloaked in disguises. One such pot, made for the use of the "kynges mageste" in 1547, was grandly upholstered to resemble a high-backed throne. By the eighteenth century chamber pots were masquerading as carved chairs and elegant cupboards; one popular rendition was a stool that sported a pile of faux books with such titles as *Mystères de Paris* or *Voyages au Pays Bas.*

These tongue-in-cheek names clearly revealed the furniture's hidden purpose to an au courant audience. In the nineteenth century ceramic toilets and chamber pots were often either lavishly decorated with floral and other motifs or hidden in thronelike chair surrounds.

Where permanent toilets existed, they were often placed in private rooms of their own. The modern convention of sink, toilet, and bathtub and/or shower in a single room is a late-nineteenth-century American concept initiated by luxury hotels. The European practice of placing the toilet in a separate room still endures in some places.

Today it is not the ability to have a steady stream of hot water on demand that astonishes us. Rather, it is the dazzling array of decorative choices we have at our disposal—our palette of opportunity stretches across cultures and across centuries.

So what does the ideal bathroom look like? When I was growing up in America in the 1950s and 1960s, bathroom design was rigidly governed by washable, waterproof surfaces, including yards of shiny ceramic tiles, vinyl wallpaper, and plastic shower curtains on plastic hooks. Every bathroom had a mirrored medicine cabinet and a plush rug/toilet seat cover set that could be easily thrown in the washing machine.

Thankfully, the cookie-cutter bathroom is a thing of the past. Now we can choose from an enormous range of fixtures and furnishings, from flea-market finds to industrial-issue flooring to vintage wall coverings. We can turn even the most ordinary space into a personal shrine of bathing, whether it be a clean, no-frills cubicle of tile and glass or a palatial bathing chamber. And because bathrooms are often the smallest room in the house, it's possible to indulge in a little fantasy decorating without breaking the bank.

13

Basic bathroom design falls into two broad categories: form follows function and form masks function. The first approach treats the utilitarian as inherently ornamental and makes no attempt to mask the practical, functional aspects of the bathroom. The fittings themselves do the decorating, and there is little superfluous ornament. Cleanliness informs the aesthetic: with shining fittings and sleek, uncluttered expanses, there is no place for grime (or even water spots) to hide, and these hygienic surfaces, in turn, can actually make us feel clean. The form-follows-function approach is perhaps epitomized by the elegant Art Deco bathrooms at Claridge's (page 53). Gleaming ceramic bathtubs, marble floors, and tiled walls are both practical and dramatic. The large watering-can shower head is fully functional, but if it were adopted into a modern bathroom design scheme it would become highly decorative, an anachronism infused with sentiment.

One excellent example of equipment-as-period-piece is the Edwardian shower-bath contraption that tops the tub on pages 49 and 52. The exposed system of pipes reveals its own inner workings, and a series of taps allows for variations in the flow of water. It's essential to the functions of the bathroom, but it's also a curiosity and forms a magnificent focal point. A more contemporary piece is a stainless-steel sink designed by London-based architect Nico Rensch. Its columnar base, inspired by a tree trunk, plays a decorative role as pure sculpture, yet it also performs the functional roles of towel rack and basin support.

The flexibility of certain fixtures can open up new design possibilities. For instance, a shower head and hose apparatus, such as the one on page 30, attaches to the floor or edge of the tub. Not only is there a certain Old World charm to such a setup, it also eliminates the need for installing a separate shower.

In some cases, interesting fittings already exist in a bathroom, but their decorative impact is lost in a jumble of textures and patterns. Here, a reductive mentality may work best. By taking nonessential elements away, you can highlight the "bones" of a room—aspects such as high ceilings, a curiously shaped window, an expanse of floor—and allow the dynamics of architecture and basic equipment to create drama. The bathroom at Manderston (page 40) has such fine proportions that it needs little more than marble walls and a sparkling white vintage tub to radiate turn-of-the-century grandeur.

The form-masks-function aesthetic de-emphasizes the bathroom's utilitarian aspects and focuses instead on its decorative elements. Popular in the eighteenth century, when ornamental objects were used to conceal the bathroom's basic functions, this design approach treats the bathroom like any other room in the house. All rules about conventional furnishings are cast aside: instead, bathrooms are made over to look like libraries, sitting rooms, or picture galleries.

Such artful camouflage is used to great effect in fashion designer Karl Lagerfeld's bathroom in Rome (page 60). With sumptuous pictures, an antique table, walls painted to simulate paneling, and charming painted chairs that hold anything from towels to books, it most resembles a cozy boudoir. The secret to its success is that, with the exception of the sink and the bathtub (encased in faux paneling), the room's furnishings and accessories could be found in any room.

In furnishing a great escapist bathroom, the found object plays a major role. When you spot a Victorian metal washstand at an auction, think twice—it could be plumbed and outfitted as a sink. The nineteenth-century chest that caught your eye at the flea market may be redundant in your bedroom, but why not employ it to store towels and toiletries in the bathroom (page 62)? You could eschew sets of terry towels and instead use time-worn tea towels, each with a unique embroidered design, as your main bathroom linens (page 111). Romantic brush sets (pages 6, 24, 70) could be destined for an honored place in the bathroom, as could the ultimate luxury: a daybed for lounging after the bath (page 74).

My personal tastes run toward the form-masks-function approach, if only because it offers more possibilities. When I restored the bathroom of my Regency house in London (see illustration on this page), I began by defining my personal feel-good factor. It wasn't difficult: I have long known that my favorite brand of escapism involves harking back to another era. So I let my imagination put me in a tub in a room with old-fashioned charm and lots of atmosphere.

For inspiration, I pored over period pattern books, prints, paint-

ings, and vintage photographs. Then I reflected on wonderful memories of travel experiences, from the deep Art Deco bathtubs at Claridge's in London (page 53) to a Victorian tub beside a crackling fire in a splendid paneled room in a French château, similar to the one on page 72.

Having decided upon the general atmosphere of my dream bathroom, I made the first two purchases: a reproduction nineteenth-century bathtub with brass and porcelain taps, and an Edwardian toilet with an elevated cistern and a chain with a porcelain pull. The sanitary ware went a long way toward establishing the room's tone, so I was ready to set out on a long and satisfying flea-market adventure.

My foraging through London, Paris, and Provence yielded great treasures. First I found a Regency corona.

THE AUTHOR'S BATHROOM.

back to another era. So I let my imagination put me in a tub in a room with old-fashioned charm and lots of atmosphere.

Though it would have originally graced a bed, in my bathroom it was perfect as a decorative device for hanging toile de Jouy curtains, whch can be pulled around the tub. (I lined the curtains with plastic to prevent

15

water damage.) Future expeditions produced a roomy, marble-topped Empire chest for storage; two pairs of sconces; a romantic dry sink in a state of disrepair; and a vintage French mirror, wonderfully beribboned but painted a hideous brown. I reclaimed the mirror by applying a faux finish and some gilding, and painted the sink and tub with a pattern of ribbons and garlands copied from a decorative panel in a famous English country house. Cupboard doors were made out of inexpensive fiberboard, then camouflaged with botanical prints hung from ribbons. The final purchase was an antique French marble fireplace found at an architectural salvage shop. At last I was able to indulge my long-awaited fantasy: a luscious bath on a wintry evening in the warm glow of firelight. I felt as though I was tucked away in another world, in another century—and I still do today.

16

No matter what your personal bath style might be, almost any material can be used on walls, floors, and other surfaces, provided you have the means to protect them from water damage. Tiles, the tried-and-true standard of bathroom surfaces, are now available in everything from basic white to hand-glazed ceramic reproductions of classical patterns to retro linoleum designs. With tiles you can re-create the watery softness of a 1930s seafoam green bathroom or the jazz-age snap of black and white optics (pages 50, 100).

Paint is a terrific tool in the bathroom as well. Color can do wonders: a basic white tub looks entirely different when it's set against a dramatic red wall. Those with creative ambitions can try more advanced paint techniques, such as trompe l'oeil murals or faux finishes; equally dramatic are decoupage treatments or do-it-yourself stencils, available in kits. Of course, wallpaper is always an option, and can offer

everything from a simple, sophisticated striped design (page 36) to a grand ribbon motif (page 78), while multiple mirrors not only make a space seem larger but also let you enjoy the whole room—even when your back is turned.

Window treatments depend on two basic requirements: privacy and light. Drapes can range from formal, full-length curtains to the tiniest wisp of vintage lace. Wooden shutters are a natural because they provide total privacy when closed, but allow the sun to stream in when open (pages 95, 98).

Most people's bathrooms are overflowing with things: soaps, lotions, potions, towels, appliances. When it comes to storage, the question is: should you conceal, or should you reveal? Each solution has its merits. Those who choose to conceal may find that chests, cabinets, and armoires work well in the bathroom. Under-sink storage can be created with cupboardlike surrounds or more simply with gathered fabric attached with Velcro. Freestanding towel racks are both useful and decorative, and don't forget the humble nightstand: in the bathroom, it's ideal for displaying all sorts of grooming equipment on top, while other utilitarian items can be stashed below.

Yet so many of the accessories needed in the bathroom are pleasingly tactile and colorful—why not show them off? A cluster of perfume bottles (pages 106 and 107), new or vintage, makes a beautiful play of light when arranged on a tabletop, and even the most prosaic items can be stunning when they're presented in volume. A single cotton ball is a stray, but a mountain of cotton balls in an antique cache-pot is a statement. You may find that some of your best decorating tools are already hidden away in your cabinets. Stacks of fresh white towels can be liberated from your linen closet, tied together with ribbons, and displayed on a petite side chair. Bars of soap piled high in a country basket not only add texture and color but smell divine. Vintage glassware, metal garden pails, baskets, odd teacups and saucers, even in/out trays designed for office use can all be employed as storage units in the bathroom. Once you've found one or more motifs to work with, the fun of collecting begins: can you imagine amassing a small army of miniature shopping bags, then hanging them on pegs to store and display cosmetics? My bathroom is filled with shiny Chanel bags as well as bags emblazoned with Gainsborough reproductions. I love to stare at them from the tub.

Because of its inherently private nature, the bathroom is the ideal place to make your wildest decorating fantasies come true. In a creative reverie you may picture yourself lolling in a tub while gazing at an endless, ever-changing seascape or soaking in theatrical opulence with gilded and painted surfaces shimmering in candlelight (page 131). Your imagination may plunge you into a deep marble pool, surrounded by the exotic splendor of an Indian palace (page 123), or find you luxuriating in a scented bath of floating flower petals in a Balinese garden.

Ultimately, it is your personal feel-good factor that will lead you to your perfect bath. On the following pages you'll find bath styles that range from the scrupulously sanitary to the dreamily decadent; with imagination and creative sleight of hand, each can be realized in your own real world. And whether you choose an exhilarating plunge into a Jacuzzi after a hard day's work or an evening-long soak in a sea of movie-star bubbles, one thing remains the same: the act of bathing is quality time you spend with yourself. In that most intimate and private of rooms, you can be absolutely free.

17

BATHING BEAUTIES

Basic Elements

Cecil Beaton once said, "What is elegance? Soap and water!" It's true: sometimes the barest essentials have an inherent beauty all their own. Case in point? Bathroom fixtures. The trio of tub, sink, and toilet, no matter how simple or complex their design, are a happy convergence of utility and aesthetics. From the traditional claw-foot tub and pedestal sink (page 30) to an opulent Jacuzzi sunk into miles of black ceramic tiles (page 27), the elements that form the bathroom's basic kit are a pleasure to the eye—and, though we may take them for granted, marvels of engineering.

Since fixtures are what make a bathroom a bathroom, smart design schemes begin with a careful consideration of sanitary ware. First question: What are your spatial constraints? If you're lucky enough to have a large bathroom, your "basic" equipment might include an oversized tub, an enclosed shower, and an antique chair for storage and/or repose (page 35). If you're faced with a tiny space, however, you'll need to come up with a tight, well-organized scheme such as the one on page 33.

Once you've determined what will fit in your dream bathroom, consult your pocketbook. New fixtures run the gamut from high-tech contraptions with multifunction nozzles to sculptural objects of art, such as the stainless-steel sink on page 25. If your budget is slim, found objects can create a bath-

room with great character. Ceramic bowls and antique chests can be transformed into charming sinks with the addition of plumbing (pages 23, 34, 36), while a secondhand tub, complete with claw-and-ball feet, can become the focal point of a cozy bathroom (pages 21, 30). Remember that sinks do not have to match tubs; the most imaginative bathrooms are acts of creation that occur between reclaimed objects and their rescuers.

As always, the most important design question involves your personal bath style. How do you want to feel in the bathroom? Does the soothing, gentle stream of a watering-can shower head appeal to you (page 38)? Would you enjoy the flexibility of a Continental-style hose attachment (page 27), or would a shower stall with a massaging downpour fulfill your needs (pages 35, 39)? The basic, no-frills kit (page 29) has a number of advantages: it creates a unified look, has a clean feeling, and lends itself to pared-down design schemes that are, as Cecil Beaton suggests, elegant in their simplicity.

Once you've made your decisions regarding basic necessities, you're well on the way toward setting the stage and creating the mood for a fabulous bathroom. Those fixtures will stay at the center of your future design decisions, and if you're good to them—and they're good to you—they'll last a lifetime or two.

PAGES 18 AND 19

What began as a boxy space in a London house has been transformed into a charming bathroom with a country look. Joanna Wood softened walls with a delicate print, added mirroring and marble to one end, then turned her touch to encasing the tub and sinks in decorative panels.

In his London flat, Count Heinrich Spreti tucked the bathroom into an almost impossibly tiny space. By cleverly manipulating mirrored panels flanking an arched window, he made both the diminutive space and the natural light seem almost vast. (LEFT)

In Dot Spikings's breezy Malibu
beach house, the floors are the
color of sand and the walls are
whitewashed to reflect sunlight.
Amid all the airiness, a cast-iron
tub takes pride of place. Though
the tub is in the Victorian style,
the room has a contemporary
look—it is defined by large
shapes, a restrained use of color,
and only the barest design details.

21

This bathroom in Shela House is on an island off the coast of Kenya. Its primitive look owes much to the fact that it is constructed of local materials, including stucco and rough-hewn timbers. A semi-enclosed shower stall, wooden shutters, and bowls placed on an ocher-colored floor all add to the room's magical African feeling.

22

This cozy corner with a certain slant of light is a converted tower room in a Scottish keep, formerly owned by Keith and Suki Schellenberg. The intimate sink area is an ideal spot for a treasured collection of antique mugs, whose delicate designs are echoed in the patterned sink. Lit by candlelight, the bathroom is especially romantic on wintry evenings. (RIGHT)

Mimmi O'Connell gave a favorite painted bowl a permanent place of honor—she turned it into a sink. The sculptural encasement has the feel of adobe, and the wall-mounted taps have a weather-beaten look—all of which contribute to the sink's primitive appeal. (BELOW)

23

This gentleman's powder room (or cloakroom, as the English call it) is in Manderston, a turn-of-the-century country house on the Scottish border. Though you may not have as spacious a bathroom, you may be able to convert a console table into something nearly as grand as this three-basin mahogany and marble sink. Crisp linens and antique brushes are the only accessories needed.

This shimmering stainless-steel sink in André Heller's Italian home is stunning in its simplicity. Featuring a deep conical basin on a columnar base, it provides the room with a striking piece of contemporary sculpture, and also makes a great pattern play by reflecting the geometric design of the floor. Because it always looks immaculate, it lends the bathroom—and the viewer—a feeling of scrupulous cleanliness. (BELOW)

A bathroom designed by Juliette Mole is filled with whimsy—right down to the tray that straddles the tub. It's where she stashes her vital bathing equipment, not the least of which is reading material. With the help of a curvaceous music stand, she can immerse herself in a good novel without fear of soggy prose. (ABOVE)

25

In this minimalist bathroom, basic elements have been combined to maximize efficiency. The no-nonsense shower stall shares a wall with a mirror, which in turn seems to double the sunlight from a square window. The sink is housed in a cube-shaped cabinet whose drawers can be accessed from three sides, while the tub throws a welcome curve at the otherwise rectilinear shapes. The room's simple floor plan is emphasized by dark flooring. (BELOW)

Sometimes, less really is more. This bathroom has been stripped to its bare essentials. Surfaces are either gleaming antiseptic white, transparent, or mirrored; working parts are treated as decorative elements, right down to the unadorned shampoo bottles and the Lucite wastebasket. The result is a pristine, polished environment. (ABOVE)

The streamlined glamour of the 1930s is captured here in a contemporary setting. Gleaming black ceramic tiles provide both a backdrop and an encasement for a thoroughly modern Jacuzzi. A single pink blossom in a frosted turquoise drinking glass adds a colorful bit of whimsy. Note the polka-dot storage boxes neatly stacked at a corner of the tub— an elegant solution to clutter.

27

The most refreshing thing about this bathroom, designed by Richard Mudditt, is its simplicity. Architectural elements lend a contemporary feeling, while basic objects in the room—the black-based tub, the reproduction radiator—function as pieces of sculpture and add period flair. Ordinary folding chairs are employed to hold everything from towels to shampoo.

German-born architect Nico Rensch has chosen to emphasize the structural elements of this bathroom. The sloping ceiling is painted bright white, in contrast to the dark floor. The Victorian-style tub is placed on terra-cotta plinths, rather than on the traditional claw-and-ball feet. In this setting even the period-style chrome towel racks look high-tech. Only the frilly window curtains add a soft touch. (BELOW)

Count Heinrich Spreti has created a clean, bold space simply by cladding surfaces in shiny white tiles. The wall above the sinks has been recessed to create a shelf; a large mirror topped by an arched brass lighting fixture underscores the contemporary look, as does the colorful painting placed high on the wall. (ABOVE)

This airy bathroom in a château in southern France gets its look of vintage grandeur from a few simple elements: footed tub, pedestal sink, rococo-style mirror, sunlight.

30

A tiny bathroom has been transformed into a grand affair in the hands of designers Osborne & Little. The sink is housed in a curved niche, which in turn is encased in a striped pattern that extends throughout the room. Shapely shelves enhance the look.

31

London mews houses—converted stables—are loaded with charm and much in demand. In spite of their appeal, they're often short on space, and bathrooms can pose a special challenge. Here, architects Child Graddon Lewis have employed a few visual tricks to transform a miniature enclave into a bathroom that feels spacious. The porthole window makes use of a space where windows are rarely found, while recessed mirrors framed with lights add depth to an otherwise ordinary wall—and create extra storage space, too.

32

Green bars of soap, white towels, bubbling water and an expanse of black marble create a study in elegance. Note the faucet emerging from the mirrored wall—it gives the impression of a magical water source, of a spring gushing forth from stone. (ABOVE)

Nico Rensch found a sleek solution to the space constraints of Robert Nadler's London mews house. Tulip wood, rich with dramatic graining, was used to emphasize the height of the diminutive room, while the sink, tub, and toilet are sunken into cool slabs of slate. (RIGHT)

33

A roomy nineteenth-century chest with faux bamboo details has been reborn as a sink in Cath Kidston's London home. The piece not only has tremendous presence but also provides ample storage space for bathroom necessities. (BELOW)

An Art Deco bathroom in Glasgow features a stout, square sink, rectangular fluorescent lights, oversized squares of green tile, and twin circular mirrors that reflect each other endlessly. It's simple geometry come to life, and simple to re-create in nearly any home. (ABOVE)

Designer Bill Bennette has infused this bathroom in an English country house with cozy, Old World charm—yet hasn't scrimped on the modern conveniences. Up-to-date fittings, including the stall shower and a built-in wall mirror, have been given period flair with the addition of molding, while the tub has been encased in paneling to match the door. At the far end of the room, floor-length drapes in an old-fashioned print frame an antique chair, completing the look of a bygone era.

35

This delightful bathroom in jewelry designer Donatella Pellini's Milanese flat is a treasure trove of found objects. A scroll-legged Empire table, transformed into a sink, is home to curios and toiletries. Lacy vintage linens are draped over an antique towel rack, and a neoclassical chair stands ready to catch the overflow—or simply provide a place of quiet repose.

Elegant Edwardian taps are a focal point of this bathtub at Lauriston Castle in Scotland, showing just how aesthetically important hardware can be. (ABOVE)

A sink at Edinburgh's Lauriston Castle is rich with majestic detail and wholly befits an aristocratic dwelling. Note the animal-head water spout, discreetly positioned below the sink's rim. (RIGHT)

37

At Mark Birley's Bath & Racquets Club, a power shower is irresistible after a vigorous game of squash. With a minimum of detail the glorious onyx-clad shower, accented by an oversized window, manages to be supremely elegant— a restorative retreat for body and soul.

Designer Joanna Wood is well aware that a functional detail as small as a shower control can make a dramatic difference. For this bathroom she chose an Edwardian-style reproduction, which attests to the fact that beauty and utility can go hand-in-hand. (ABOVE)

39

A shower stall in a London flat is sleek and clean, a high-tech convergence of glass, chrome, and marble. It's anything but cold, however: the dark sienna color of the polished stone casts a fiery, inviting glow. (LEFT)

PURE AND SIMPLE
Form Follows Function

In the bathroom form and function are inextricably linked. Simply by leaving utilitarian elements exposed and laying the structure bare, you can give a bathroom enormous style. This form-follows-function approach glorifies the room's purpose. Its aesthetic is sleek and streamlined because ornament is intrinsic, never additive. Imagine plain white fixtures . . . walls and floors covered with white ceramic builder's tiles . . . fluffy white towels on a simple rack . . . a cotton bathrobe hung on a peg. The result is a bathroom that feels light, bright, and ultraclean.

Of course, the form-follows-function approach isn't always so minimalist. Functional equipment, no matter what period it dates from, can be extremely decorative. In a bathroom at the Halkin Hotel, for example, structural features have been turned into decorative assets. Its slanted ceiling, understated black granite tub, silvery towel rack, and pristine bars of soap all have a period feel, and they conspire to create a sophisticated look that is much more than the sum of its parts (page 51).

Building materials are an important element of any room, and nowhere is this more true than in the bathroom. A mixture of plaster and cement, molded by Mimmi O'Connell into curved sink and bath surrounds, lends a feeling of local craft traditions to modern fixtures (pages 42 and 43). Andrew Wadsworth chose stainless steel to make a unique statement in the bathroom on page 44.

By working with unusual materials, you, too, can create a look that's striking but never fussy. How about industrial-strength rubber tiles on the walls? Vintage linoleum on floors and tabletops? Sheets of brightly colored corrugated metal can become a shower enclosure; a slab of granite can become a counter.

With a clever arrangement of high-contrast tiles you can create dramatic patterns, much like the extravagant Art Deco designs at Claridge's (pages 46, 53). There is not a single picture on Claridge's walls, yet the tiles, marble floors, and oversized taps create imposing rooms of great elegance.

A bathroom's more personal equipment—mirrors, towel racks, soap trays—also offer great decorative opportunities. In the Parisian bathroom on page 57, three oval mirrors unify an assortment of old and new fixtures. Wendy Harrop's former London bathroom (page 58) looks for all the world like a seaside retreat, thanks to baskets and wood-handled brushes against a painted floor. In Eliel Saarinen's Finnish bathroom, cabinets faced with mirrors provide storage and act as part of a built-in vanity (page 59). In each case, accessories add visual interest while fulfilling important bath-time functions.

Whatever your tastes, the following pages will show you how durable materials and essential equipment can come together to make a bathroom that's at once unique and utterly functional.

41

PAGES 40 AND 41

This bathroom at Manderston, an Edwardian country house in Scotland, contrasts a delicately painted antique chair and step against an expanse of cool, smooth marble. The hanging servants' pulls are reminders of days gone by.

Mimmi O'Connell has taken the simplest of materials—cement and plaster—and molded them into a curved cabinet. The soft corner and plain white paint play counterpoint to the carved mirror and leafy sconces unearthed on a shopping foray. (RIGHT)

42

There are found objects . . . and then there are found materials. The antique terra-cotta tiles in a Mallorcan room designed by Port of Call transform a mere shower floor into a delightful treat for the feet. (ABOVE)

In the same bathroom, a whitewashed platform is not only visually appealing, it's four times practical: (1) It provides a convenient step up to the tub; (2) it's a stage for brightly painted bowls; (3) it raises the height of the tub so that a garden view can be enjoyed; and (4) its organic shape breaks the rigid geometry of the bathroom and lends it a hand-crafted charm. (RIGHT)

43

In Andrew and Julie Wadsworth's former London home, function reigns. Using stainless steel, he created a contrast between severe surfaces and the sexy curves of an antique footed tub. The result is not unlike a classical sculpture displayed in a modern gallery.

44

The gentleman's cloakroom at Manderston features an Edwardian toilet with a wooden seat atop a ceramic base. Decorative elements are kept to a minimum; miles of immaculate marble make the statement.

In the steam room at the Bath & Racquets Club in London, nearly every surface is covered by huge slabs of dramatically patterned marble. Simple mahogany doors—and, of course, the steam itself—provide inviting contrasts to the Spartan marble benches and shining floors. (LEFT AND BELOW)

47

When Tessa Kennedy was commissioned by Claridge's to give this Art Deco bathroom a facelift, she equipped it with all the creature comforts one would expect in the 1990s—and still retained the old-fashioned charm for which the hotel is renowned. The marble sink is pure elegance, and the etched-and-frosted-glass door retains a period feeling while assuring total privacy. Small but essential details, such as the Art Deco light above the sink and the heated towel rack—to ensure that a toasty towel is never far from reach—bring Claridge's illustrious past back to life. (FACING PAGE)

California antiques dealer Jerry Welling's bathroom is slick, streamlined, and utterly Art Deco. The tiled walls and floor not only play up the room's architecture but also can be washed down in minutes. Alternating colors and shapes enliven the surfaces, and tiles decorated with high-contrast motifs are the crowning glory. Archways, framing both the bath and shower, add a touch of softness to the room's stark linearity. The result is a feeling of gleaming cleanliness, supported by the pristine pedestal sink and an industrial-strength ceiling light. (ABOVE AND RIGHT)

48

In this stylish London bathroom, designed by Peter Wood & Partners, objects borrowed from different periods converge with great ease. The key to its success is its simple color scheme and its emphasis on utility, highlighted by twin pedestal sinks, Art Deco— style mirrors, and the elaborate antique shower apparatus.

49

It's simple, it's clean, it's chic. In this London bathroom, a vertical tile pattern acts like an architectural element, creating visual columns that seem to hold the room up and tie its functional components together. Plain white fixtures appear to float above the black floor.

The dramatic swoop of a flying arch softens the hard-edged beauty of this bathroom in the Halkin Hotel, London. Its shape is emphasized by contrasting surfaces and echoed by a rounded countertop. Marble-clad walls and floors, polished to a mirrorlike gleam, seem to double the depth of the room.

Le Corbusier wrote, "A house is a machine for living in." This turn-of-the-century shower apparatus is a case in point, and the central focus of a bathroom designed by Peter Wood & Partners. Though it looks like an elaborate chrome crib, its impressive system of pipes and taps are all working parts laid bare. It is at once fascinating and practical, a glorious tribute to the beauty of function.

It's no wonder that Kensington Green is considered one of London's premier addresses. This bathroom, with its great expanses of richly patterned marble, upholds a tradition of grand elegance. Note how the mirrored cabinet, placed at right angles to the sink, adds accessible storage while lending visual interest by changing the spatial impression of the room. (BELOW)

53

This bathroom at Claridge's in London is a jewel of Art Deco design and a fine example of the form-follows-function aesthetic. Simple yellow tiles look grand edged in black. A no-frills tub seems miles deep. Shining marble floors, matte marble sinks, and the simple geometry of a coved ceiling all contribute to its character; even the massive taps, decorative yet efficient-looking, add to the overall splendor. (ABOVE)

The simplest way to decorate a bathroom is to cover it in tile. Tiled surfaces are easy to clean and stand up to water. They are also rich with decorative possibilities, as this room, designed by Bingham Land, attests. Marble tiles with a vertical grain have been interspersed with strong, striped tiles, creating a bathroom that Mondrian himself would have been eager to bathe in.

54

London designer John Stefanidis is masterful
when it comes to creating luxury and glamour
in simple settings. Here, a black granite tub
is pure theater in a bare white room. The
gleaming chrome of taps and towel rack echoes
the stone's high polish, while the stage of the
tub itself is graced with personal props,
including a pale wooden scrub brush and
cream-colored soaps.

55

A simple bathroom is transformed into a soothing environment by London designers Osborne & Little. Tiles, alternating in subtle tones, are topped by a decorative border. A contemporary wooden rack is layered with white ribbed towels and rustic country linens. The circular wall mirror, orbited by a pull-out arm, breaks the horizon of the wall and echoes the soft curves of the sink and the sconce. (LEFT)

Painted walls, bare floorboards, and wooden frames around tubs and cabinets are some of the simple elements that make the bathroom in this Parisian apartment special. The antique dressing table lends a strong period flavor, and its looking glass is mimicked by the mirrors on opposing walls, giving pleasing continuity to the room. (FACING PAGE)

This bathroom in Wendy Harrop's former London house has all the breeziness of an oceanfront cottage. Walls are whitewashed; raised floors are painted the color of weather-beaten driftwood; a sunken tub is flanked by built-in shelves that display a collection of many-textured things. Besides platforms that seem just right for stretching out on, the room's beachy feel is expressed by a rustic basket piled high with freshly laundered towels and natural sponges. (FACING PAGE)

Eliel Saarinen engaged in a delightful play of geometric shapes when he designed this Finnish bathroom. A vanity of sorts has been created out of a standard full-length mirror flanked by vertical cabinets whose mirrored surfaces have been divided into panes by tracing bars. A semicircular chair mirrors the vanity arrangement—both literally and figuratively. (RIGHT)

BEAUTY TREATMENTS

Form Masks Function

Some of the loveliest bathrooms don't seem like bathrooms at all. They may in fact resemble a library, a boudoir filled with antiques, a sitting room, or a private art gallery. The form-masks-function approach to design takes its cue from a time when jewel-box bathrooms were coveted status symbols. It recalls an era when functional equipment was often hidden behind ornamental facades, or, if left in full view, decorated to the point where illusion overwhelmed reality. Every surface and object presented an opportunity for decorative expression.

In contrast to the form-follows-function aesthetic, the dress-up approach invites you to become a couturier and create a costume for your bathroom in any style from any period. One way to design an atmospheric bathroom is to start with a simple white ceramic or acrylic tub and build an enclosure for it. This can be constructed from inexpensive wood paneling, then imaginatively finished. Looks can range from faux marble (page 73) to rustic pine (page 74), or panels can simply be painted to match an overall color scheme (page 114). An alcove is even more dramatic because it adds a strong architectural element and creates a total bathing environment (page 69). Tubs can be painted, too. An original design painted on the bathtub in the late Laura Ashley's Brussels home looks like it jumped off the pages of a Victorian pattern book (page 65).

The toilet is another ideal candidate for camouflage. In the eighteenth and nineteenth centuries toilets were often concealed by chairlike surrounds. This tradition can be revived, as witnessed by the caned disguise on page 70 and the high-backed Regency "chair" on page 62, which looks as though it lost its way while trying to escape from the dining room.

For those who equate the tub with relaxation, bedlike drapes and dressings may hold a special appeal. They soften harsh fixtures, transforming bathtubs from clean machines into decadent retreats. The secret is that a lavish expanse of draped fabric is also practical: it can double as a shower curtain (page 64).

Some of the great escapist bathrooms rely heavily on found objects. A vintage chair placed near the bathtub (pages 71, 72) automatically changes the context of a room, turning it from a place of utility to a place of luxury. Collections of pictures, such as the ones on pages 60, 63, and 66, invite bathers to linger, while stacks of books (page 4) practically ensure a long soak.

The rooms on the following pages are deliberately alluring. With decorative euphemism, metaphor, and a touch of whimsy, they beckon you to enter and be pampered.

PAGES 60 AND 61

Approached by a spiral staircase that winds down from the attic boudoir, Karl Lagerfeld's bathroom in Rome is dripping with vintage style. The walls are painted with a faux-bois finish that simulates antique paneling, and hung with pictures one might expect to find in a grand sitting room. A painted chair provides a perch for bath-time reading; even the tub is neatly clad in a trompe l'oeil finish. It's a room custom-made for lingering.

At Lauriston Castle in Scotland, the eighteenth-century tradition of the chaise percée *is evident —the toilet is imaginatively disguised as a fine French armchair. An antique chest and Chippendale stool are on hand to hold reading material or extra towels, making the room a welcoming place to relax and reflect.* (RIGHT)

This cozy bathroom, cosseted away in the Welsh countryside, gets much of its charm from warm red walls. With a freestanding tub, vintage photographs, family portraits and the promise of a roaring fire, the room is an invitation to bathe—perhaps all evening. (BELOW)

63

Designer Richard Mudditt has created a warm, masculine atmosphere in his London bathroom. The airy ceiling is echoed by the natural sisal flooring, while the matte black of the tub's base disappears against the dark paneling and fireplace. In the middle of it all, the unusual freestanding faucet and gleam of white porcelain look positively sculptural. (ABOVE)

The late Laura Ashley draped, papered, and populated her bathroom with pattern, color, and antiques until it looked more like a sumptuous Victorian sitting room than a bathroom. The painted tub, mahogany-encased sink, and nineteenth-century-style throne chair disguising the toilet all make this a delightful room in which to soak and dream, especially by candlelight. Note the high pull-chain toilet tank, adding to the feeling of a century gone by. (FACING PAGE)

Another view of the bathroom in Laura Ashley's Brussels home shows the lengths to which patterns can be used to create mood. The small print on the walls contrasts with paisley prints on shower curtains and windows, while the tub, decorated with nineteenth-century motifs, ties the color palette together. (RIGHT)

David Bennett's bathroom, nestled in the English countryside, looks more like a private art gallery than a place to wash up. Though the Victorian-style tub is an immediate giveaway, one has the feeling that the room's real function is to house an eclectic collection of pictures, which range from an antique land deed to a Bernard Buffet lithograph. The shelf beside the tub and the antique chest, which is used for storage, add to the unbathroomlike atmosphere.

66

In fashion designer Valentino's London residence, a Victorian-style tub has been seductively concealed with softly gathered fabric. For designer Roger Banks-Pye of Sibyl Colefax and John Fowler, hiding the tub was just the beginning: he then filled the room with treasures that would make it seem more like a gentleman's sitting room than a bathroom. The paneled sink surround, antique mirror flanked by sconces, and selection of Chinese porcelain all conspire to make bath time a feast for the senses.

67

Glynn Boyd Harte's bathroom is a spacious place filled with light and air. A leaf-patterned paper is repeated in sheer drapes on enormous windows. Bare floorboards, a rustically finished tub, an exposed closet, and a stack of vintage books all recall the Georgian era. (FACING PAGE)

Sam and Jeannie Chesterton designed an imaginative paneled alcove—perhaps inspired by traditional sleeping alcoves—to house their roomy tub. Storage cabinets are hidden behind the raised and fielded paneling, while a washstand with ceramic bowl looks as if it's been there since the nineteenth century. (RIGHT)

Piers von Westenholz is both an antiques dealer and a designer, and this bathroom, in his English country home, reflects both passions. Simple painted wainscoting blankets the room, creating an environment that's absolutely right for a country gentleman. The toilet is hidden beneath a caned chair with a high back for comfort as well as style. The monogrammed grooming set, displayed on a side table, is the kind of collectible that's ideal for the well-dressed bathroom. (LEFT)

As befits a country house designed by Lutyens, Vicky Rothcoe has infused this inviting bathroom with old-fashioned charm. Decorative touches include Delft tiles facing the fireplace, a carved-mahogany pot cupboard, a period chair, antique mirrors, and a mix-and-match collection of blue-and-white transfer-printed pottery, displayed on the mantelpiece and pressed into service at the tub's edge to hold soaps and sundries. (FACING PAGE)

Peeking around a wall of French paneling in Veuve Clicquot's elegant Hôtel du Marc in Champagne country, one would expect to see a room with a view, but not a room with a view and a tub. Here, the sitting room aesthetic is fully carried through to the bathroom. A crystal chandelier, a gilded antique table dripping with flowers, a period French chair bearing a stack of towels, and a patterned carpet make an ever-so-civilized bathing salon.

72

In jewelry designer Donatella Pellini's Belle Epoque apartment in Milan, a bathroom is graced with a floor-to-ceiling window paned in pale circles of glass. An antique table and chair create a perfect place for grooming rituals; a faux-marble-clad bathtub is a perfect place to soak and dream. (ABOVE)

Is it a mirror image? In Donatella Pellini's bathroom, style repeats itself. Twin sinks with matte gunmetal gray surrounds have a 1940s look, while a pair of arched mirrors, reflecting into a pair of square mirrors, have an older, warmer feel. Matching chests, faux-marble dividers, and antique lamps all combine to create an eclectic bathroom of great style and comfort. (RIGHT)

73

In Andrea de Montal's former home in the English countryside, the bathroom's generous proportions allow it to double as a delightful sitting room. The secret to its success is that the tub is dressed to look like country pine furniture, making it quite at home with the rustic painted daybed. It is truly a place for all-day escapes from the worries of the world. (FACING PAGE)

Maybe you haven't been lucky enough to inherit a romantic Scottish keep. But that doesn't mean you can't have the same rustic beauty of Keith and Suki Schellenberg's former residence. First, try covering your bathtub with stripped-down wood. Then add old country beams, shutters, and cabinets, and you will be well on your way to creating a charming keep of your own. (RIGHT)

75

BATH ROBES
Surface Treatments

If you were brought up to believe that bathroom walls and floors were required to be waterproof and scrubable, the bathrooms on the following pages might open your mind. Though water damage is a genuine concern, workable surfaces have evolved beyond the unvarying tiled walls and vinyl shower curtains of yesteryear. Today—as it was in the early days of the private bathroom—walls can be stylishly decorated with anything from swags of fabric to elaborate murals.

Walls and floors set the decorative tone of a room, tie its elements together, and infuse it with atmosphere. The bathroom on page 80 shows how applying a textured paint to faux-paneled walls and a bath surround can create immediate unity of design simply and inexpensively. Hung with botanical prints, the small room makes a strong statement. On the more elaborate end of the spectrum, witness the boldly striped environment on page 78 or the patterned walls of Elsa Peretti's bathroom (page 87). Enveloped in color and pattern, each room has an unmistakable identity.

Natural materials like marble and wood can lend high style to even the most ordinary bathroom. On page 92, pale blonde wood sets a warm tone; on page 95, a combination of mahogany panels and faux-tortoiseshell walls creates depth and drama. Marble is indisputably elegant, as the bathrooms on pages 88 and 89 demonstrate, but what's nice for those on a slim budget is that

marble, wood, and a world of materials in between—lapis lazuli, tortoiseshell, malachite, and stone blocking, to name a few—can be approximated with paint. The power of paint is spectacularly expressed in the classical-style bath on page 94, which gets its drama from contrasting faux-marble finishes. In the late Rudolf Nureyev's apartment, paint becomes a viny pattern on a distressed-finish wall (page 76), while a cheery stencil pattern personalizes a bathroom on Corfu (page 83). You can try your hand at trompe l'oeil and fool the eye with something simple—faux fabric, panels, or ribbons—or something more complicated, such as an entire panoramic landscape on the walls or cherubs cavorting on the ceiling.

During the eighteenth century, people often collected prints as souvenirs of places they had visited. When they returned home, it was the height of fashion to paste them on the walls and link them with decorative borders. The same effect can be achieved today with postcards, photographs, images from magazines, even vintage labels. These can be framed and hung with ribbons (page 82), offset with reproduction borders (page 91), or applied directly to the walls and covered with a coat of clear varnish.

Glass bricks, painted wainscoting (pages 70, 105), plaster wall ornaments (page 93), inset mirrors, animal-patterned wallpaper, hand-painted tiles—the key to great bathroom surfaces is imagination.

PAGES 76 AND 77

In the late Rudolf Nureyev's Paris apartment, paint is used to delicious, delirious effect. Viny floral designs wind below the chair rail, while faux marble creates a background for a collection of eighteenth- and nineteenth-century nudes fit for a major museum. A cast-iron tub provides the perfect perch from which to gaze.

Sandra Ankarcrona of Coxe Design created an all-over fantasy environment for the bathroom in her London house. The ceiling, walls, and even the radiator are covered in a ribbony pattern, giving the illusion that the room is under a festive tent. A Victorian-style chair holds a fringed bolster, while the plumbing of the wall-mounted sink is obscured behind the intricate arabesque patterns of a metal base. (RIGHT)

78

When Mimmi O'Connell was asked to design this diminutive bathroom in picture dealer Stephanie Hoppen's New York apartment, she relied on details to make the statement. A fabric shower curtain with a contrasting border and opulent tie-backs set a sitting room theme; with the addition of a tiny side table filled with soaps, sundries, antique perfume bottles, and a candlestick lamp, the space was transformed into a delightful jewel box.

79

In this inviting bathroom designed by Antony Little of Osborne & Little,
colored images of wildlife, hung on pale gray walls, add a touch of
the outdoors. Though the walls may look paneled, it's a clever illusion:
they're actually framed by molding strips. (ABOVE)

The same Osborne & Little bathroom looks startlingly different with a
change of color. This view reveals a dramatic purple-paned stained-glass
window, casting magical light. One reason that the tub seems to fit so neatly
in its niche is that it's encased in a painted panel that matches the walls—
in this case, a deep, smoky tone. (BELOW)

All the charm of provincial France was transplanted across the Atlantic for this delightful bathroom, created by Pierre Serrurier and Imogen Taylor of the London design firm of Sibyl Colefax & John Fowler. Walls covered in a pastoral toile de Jouy conjure up the romance of the countryside, while the deliciously deep tub adds glamour. Several shopping sprees in Paris yielded the antique tables, accessories, and marble floor tiles.

81

Fee zu Solms-Baruth's London home is adorned with all of her favorite things. In the bathroom, pale yellow walls edged with ornamental borders create a cozy backdrop for a collection of antique plates and framed prints. Though eclectic, the decorative objects are unified by the ribbons from which they're hung, and that theme is repeated in the beribboned mirror that crowns the sink. The room pays testimony to the fun of antiquing, and the ways in which diverse treasures can bring loads of personality to the bath. (FACING PAGE)

Sunny tiles topped by a breezy, leafy stencil pattern lend an open-air feeling to this bathroom at San Stefano on Corfu. The cheery yellow of the tiles has been applied to the simple wooden chair and the trim of the rustic closet. Original ceiling beams, painted bright white, add to the overall charm. (RIGHT)

83

When a particularly fruitful scavenger hunt yielded a nineteenth-century wrought-iron washstand, the owners of Talaysac, a manor house in southwestern France, gleefully carted it home and installed it in the bathroom. Before the weekend was over it was filled with lotions, potions, fresh flowers, and a hurricane lamp, which lends a glow of romance to evening baths. The curvaceous folding screen was discovered on a Sunday outing to a bric-a-brac fair (a constant temptation in rural France). It immediately found a home alongside the tub. Recovered with a striped canvas and hung with a collection of nineteenth-century Scottish prints, it creates a fascinating backdrop. The screen has other uses, too: not only can clothes be flung upon it, but it can be moved around the room at will, to prevent drafts or add a bit of privacy.

(ABOVE AND RIGHT)

No creature comforts were ever spared in Juliette Mole's former London houseboat. Even the bathroom is decked out with swagged curtains, a sconce for candlelight bathing, and an elegant gallery of pictures. Combined with more rustic features—the barn-boarded ceiling, cupboards, and tub surround—it makes the idea of bathing on the water seem appealing indeed.

85

Contrasting patterns above and below a chair rail bring surprising harmony to a small room. Designed for Elsa Peretti by Renzo Mongiardino, this bathroom is dominated by a dramatic circle of mirror—which maximizes the late afternoon sunlight—and by a warm color scheme that borrows from the palette of the surrounding Italian countryside.

Once again, pattern is used to great effect in another of Elsa Peretti's bathrooms. Here, three similar patterns become ever smaller as they move toward the ceiling, creating the illusion of height. A Venetian mirror amplifies the effect.

At Pennyhill Park, massive blocks
of marble with contrasting borders
on floor and walls create a
sumptuous look. The regal
air carries through to the
ceiling, which is outfitted with
ornamental moldings. Ready-
made copies of decorative ceiling
treatments are available in many
hardware stores; when given a
coat of paint, they literally add
a crowning touch to any
bathroom. Another special
feature at Pennyhill Park is the
monogrammed towels. If you don't
live in a house grand enough to
have a name, why not personalize
your towels with embroidered
initials or your name?

88

This bathroom, designed by John Stefanidis, is both supremely glamorous and exceedingly simple. It relies on a dramatic expanse of densely veined pink marble, which in turn is reflected in a wall of mirrors. If you want your bathroom to look as though its materials were custom-mined for you in a famous Italian quarry, try painting them with a marble finish and adding mirrors bought by the yard at a hardware store.

When Mlinaric, Henry and Zervudachi Ltd. was commissioned to design this bijou of a bathroom in a London mews house, he capitalized on the intrinsic charm of its irregular architecture. A subtle texture, created with paint, covers the walls and ceiling and gives the room the feeling of a cozy, tented space. (BELOW)

Another view of this bathroom shows a clever trick of paint: the molding around the doorway has been finished to match the marble countertop and tub. Though traditionalists may tell you that contrasting textures and patterns are too busy for a small space, the various earth tones of this room blend harmoniously. Even if you were just walking down the hallway, wouldn't you like to catch a glimpse of an enclave as soft and pretty as this? (ABOVE)

In a London bathroom designed by Anne Griggs, the eighteenth-century tradition of the print room comes to life. In this case, the "prints" are pasted directly onto a delicately patterned wallpaper, then "framed" with decorative borders. The result is an engaging, romantic backdrop for gleaming modern fixtures.

91

Nico Rensch has used pale
blonde wood in this bathroom to
create an environment rich in
architectural detail, yet with a
simple, contemporary air. The
wooden paneling is more than
decorative, however: secret wall
panels open onto storage areas,
while one polished wooden plank
lifts to reveal a toilet. Even the
terry-upholstered banquette isn't
what it seems—its lid opens to
provide more storage.

We've all heard of making a cameo appearance, but have you ever thought of putting a collection of cameos in the bathroom? In this space designed by Londoner Stephen Ryan, a narrow strip of wall becomes a vertical gallery. Though your own cameo collection may be made of inexpensive plaster, or even painted right on the wall, it can, like this one, set a unique theme. A lavish bouquet of lilies is another atmospheric touch: the flowers add visual drama, and steamy baths coax forth their beguiling aroma.

93

This grand classical-style bath isn't classical at all: it's the creation of London designer Lady Victoria Waymouth. Walls are painted with a faux-marble finish and framed in contrasting tones to set off a collection of English silhouettes and drawings. Only the shade can safely be called Roman; bathers can raise it to let in a garden view, or lower it when privacy is desired.

94

Some of the most exciting moments of decorating occur when found objects gain a new life by being placed out of context. In this London bathroom, designer Anouska Hempel has brought together a classical sculpture, an antique covered dish, and a painted mug, and perched them all at the edge of the tub. This grouping of the owner's personal possessions makes the room his own. With a well-stocked antique magazine rack nearby, bath time is guaranteed to be at least as intellectually and aesthetically rewarding as time spent in the drawing room. Masculine mahogany paneling lends this gentleman's bathroom a distinct clublike elegance. The walls above the chair rail have been given a glossy tortoiseshell finish that richly offsets a small gallery of historical prints. (ABOVE AND RIGHT)

9 5

Rather than making his bathroom
look like a bathroom, David
Bennett treated it more like a
study or library. A collection of
paintings and prints, antique
mirrors, a caned chair, and a sink
encased in country paneling are
all stylish details that divert the
look of the room from its
functional purpose.

96

Stone-block walls and an enormous skylight bring the natural world into this bathroom designed by Luis Charmat. Whether flooded with sunlight or filled with the drumming sounds of a spring rain, this room's mood is shaped by the hour of the day and the ever-changing patterns of the seasons. A neoclassical chair provides both a stylistic surprise and a nice place to sit and enjoy the weather.

At Blakes Hotel in London, bathing is a dramatic affair. This room, designed by couturier Anouska Hempel, gets its theatricality from the dark, glossy paint covering its walls and moldings. Cleverly positioned spotlights make fixtures seem as if they're glowing, while the wooden floor, laid in an octagonal pattern, makes visual sense of the room's high contrasts. (LEFT)

In this London bathroom, a clean sweep of open space is articulated by a diamond-patterned wooden floor. The bare window and the marble-clad surfaces are warmed by old-fashioned rattan furnishings and an exuberant spray of wildflowers. (FACING PAGE)

BEAUTY SECRETS
Storage Solutions

No matter how large your bathroom may be, it is probably the smallest room in the house. Yet it is called upon to store an inordinate number of things, from a host of grooming and beauty supplies to paper goods, appliances, and stacks of towels. Needless to say, finding a place for everything can be a challenge.

Basically, there are two broad approaches to bathroom storage: concealing and revealing. You can either hide everything behind closed doors for an organized, uncluttered look, or capitalize on the intrinsic beauty of lotions, potions, and linens, and place them plainly in sight.

When it comes to concealment, cabinets and cupboards are the obvious hiding places. Less traditional are sliding doors that camouflage a whole wall of storage space (page 103 right), and under-sink areas imaginatively housed in sculpted surrounds (page 103 left). Salvaged furniture can also be put to beautiful use. In Paola Navone's home a rustic cabinet stands tall (page 108); steps away, a striking folk-art chest provides additional storage (page 109).

You can also devise storage systems of your own. Reclaimed materials, such as antique painted doors or fragments of old paneling, can add infinite charm to a homemade cupboard. Or take a tip from Christophe Gollut: he designed an ingenious built-in armoire that showcases rows of shoes (page 113). In spirit, the cabinet bridges the "conceal" and "reveal" approaches: though the system is sleek and orderly, the shoes are clearly meant to be seen.

When you choose to reveal your bathroom's secrets, storage becomes a visual game. Shelves can hold glittering glassware, brushes, and photographs (pages 100, 110), while a tub's edge can become an intimate gallery of the perfumer's art (page 106). Nearly any kind of container can hold linens, shampoo bottles, and soaps. Flea markets may turn up vintage biscuit tins, big rattan baskets, clunky glass mason jars, garden pails, even hotel ashtrays.

When floor or counter space is tight, try stacking containers. Boxes from hats, shoes, or dresses—perhaps covered in wallpaper—make lively towers in which to stash things. Plastic laundry baskets, filled with freshly folded and beribboned linens, can rest one atop another. Wire trays, too, can be put to stylish use.

Among all the stashing and stacking there is, finally, the will to drape. An antique hat rack might sport a bright kimono, or a series of hooks could host a colorful gathering of towels (page 104 left). Freestanding racks are ideal for showcasing linens (pages 104 right, 111), and an old table, draped in white cotton, may create its own hidden storage (page 107).

Whether you are a concealer or a revealer, or somewhere in between, the following pages will prove that there is, in fact, a place for everything.

PAGES 100 AND 101

A stark black-and-white palette,
a clever manipulation of tile and
mirror, and an emphasis on slick
surfaces are what make this
Parisian bathroom so stylish.
A pedestal sink is flanked by
Lucite-and-metal cabinets, while
a contemporary heated towel rack
(at right) adds a sculptural
element. Everything in the room is
both chic and ultrafunctional.

1 0 2

In old houses it can be difficult to
construct a powder room without
chopping up an otherwise well-
proportioned space. An existing
closet may hold the answer. The
owners of Talaysac in south-
western France put a rustic closet
to ingenious use by installing a
sink, cabinet, and mirror,
anchoring a towel rack to the
inside of the door, and placing a
toilet adjacent to it. The result is
a darling guest bathroom that
doesn't compromise the room's
original dimensions. (RIGHT)

At St. Nicholas Abbey, a Barbados plantation house, sliding cabinet doors hide a multitude of sins. The doors themselves are perfectly camouflaged; they're fashioned from the same white wainscoting as the walls. Hooks attached to a strip of ordinary molding make a more obvious place to hang one's straw hat, or beach towel. (BELOW)

In this bathroom designed by Port of Call, a sturdy Mallorcan table provides storage as well as decorative interest. With three tiers, it is an ideal place to perch towels, toiletries, and, in this case, a collection of local blue glass bottles filled with everything from mineral water to perfume. (ABOVE)

103

104

Stylist Fanny Ward has made this hand-hewn towel rack look as though it's occupied this simple wainscoted bathroom forever. It makes a natural showcase for country linens—from homespun checks to a white-on-white coverlet—and for sweet-smelling sachets that are much too pretty to hide in a drawer. (BELOW)

Instead of having a matched set of towels, Richard Mudditt bought one in each of his favorite hues. Softly faded by laundering, they create a chromatic display when hung from simple brass hooks on a plain white wall. (ABOVE)

A charming vintage mirror makes a pretty and oh-so-useful place to store towels. This was an object "found" by Joanne Creveling when she acquired the house. She simply refreshed it with a wash of white paint and added hooks for hanging additional linens.

105

106

When turning her imagination toward
storage solutions, Mimmi O'Connell decided
to highlight the inherent beauty of toiletries.
In this Mallorcan bathroom, bottles of
perfumes and bath oils and essences provide
a gallery of bath-time possibilities. (LEFT)

Some beauty secrets are too scintillating to
remain untold. Another view of Mimmi
O'Connell's Mallorcan creation reveals the
extended shape of the tub, achieved by
continuing its plaster surround to form a
ledge beneath the window, where precious
bottles of scent catch the light. The sensuous
lines of the softly curving plaster are picked
up by the curtains and the draped vanity,
where more treasures are prettily displayed.
(FACING PAGE)

Against the cerulean blue tiles of architect Paola Navone's Milanese bathroom, one storage solution stands out: it's a rustic cabinet painted dusty pink. Doors, lined with translucent mesh, open on drawers and shelves stacked with towels and toiletries. The oversized perfumers' bottles on top lend an exotic touch. A metal basin placed beguilingly on the floor holds soaps, and a hat stand topped by a primitive figure holds fringed towels.

108

A folk-art prelude to the bath: in Paola Navone's apartment, just a step away from the bathroom, a primitive painted chest provides a striking decorative moment, as well as ample storage. A host of tiny figurines looks on. (ABOVE)

The design firm Osborne & Little centered this bathroom on a vivid Arts and Crafts piece. A wooden base, inlaid with floral motifs, has a drawer and a tiny cabinet for storage. The marble top and tiled backboard are highly decorative yet impervious to water damage. Contemporary tile and a cool, dark color on the wall bring out the warmth of the antique wood while creating a bridge between the late nineteenth century and the 1990s. (BELOW)

109

In this glossy London bathroom designed by Peter Wood & Partners, lotions and potions are the focal point. They're placed on a tall column of open shelving, backed with mirrors for extra glitter. A glass-and-chrome cart on wheels ensures that such essentials as toilet paper and a telephone are always close at hand. (LEFT)

In the bathroom of Mimmi O'Connell's former Tuscan farmhouse, an antique, two-tiered folding stand makes a fascinating towel rack. The towels themselves become decorative elements, too; her collection ranges from red-and-white kitchen towels to antique linens. A nineteenth-century armchair is just the place to toss clothes—as the figure in the painting seems about to do—and a stool provides another spot on which to drape towels and quilts. (FACING PAGE)

110

A divine place to recline is also a simple space for storage. This minimalist composition, in a London mews house designed by Christina Mathieu and architects Child Graddon Lewis, plays crisp white upholstery against fluffy white towels. Some are hung from hooks in a niche; others form a neat stack on a stool.

112

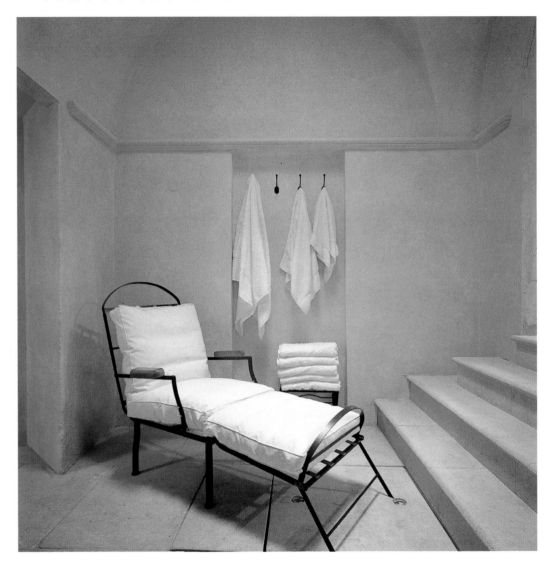

The pièce de résistance in this London bathroom is the shoe cabinet. Designed by Christophe Gollut, it most resembles an armoire, but its pierced doors fitted with glass reveal row upon row of impeccably polished footwear. Beyond its merits as an imaginative storage solution, the cabinet adds masculine style while showcasing a collection far too handsome to be closeted away.

113

It comes as no surprise that Janet Fitch is a jewelry designer, because she has accessorized her bathroom in the same way as one would adorn oneself with baubles. Decorative touches include a stenciled shell border above the chair rail, a Victorian slipper chair, and an ornamental kilim on the floor. Surfaces are subtle, but none are left untouched; note the faux wood graining on the tub surround and cabinets, framed with borders to simulate inlaid paneling. (LEFT)

When decorating a bathroom in Scotland, "love in a cold climate" is an appropriate theme to keep in mind. This bathroom in a Georgian house in Edinburgh combines intimate warmth with the majesty of a gentleman's club. Built-in wood armoires with a timeworn patina, an oversized Georgian-style mirror bathed in soft light, and an assortment of antique accessories all speak of the lost charms of a bygone era. It's pure romance in any sort of weather. (FACING PAGE)

114

MAKING A SPLASH

Fantasy Bathrooms

The bathroom is an intimate, private space. It's also a place of total relaxation and escape, and lends itself perfectly to flights of fancy and fantasy. Since the bathroom's purpose is self-indulgence, you can—and should—give free reign to your imagination and transform the space into a magical environment in which you feel completely soothed and entirely special.

Fantasies are very personal. They might be extravagant, or they might be sweet and simple, but they are always the dream that spirits you away from the familiarities of day-to-day life. If you're a high-rise city-dweller, your bath fantasies might put you in a wooden tub in a country cottage or under an outdoor shower near a sun-bleached porch, with pounding surf and whispering dune grass all around. If your daily life is stressful and hectic, you might seek an oasis of greenery, of fragrant orchids and steaming waters, like the opulent environment on pages 118 and 119. Your imagination may take you halfway around the world and steep you in the pleasures of a maharajah's bath (page 123), or plunge you into a pool that seems to be under a canopy of stars at the very center of an exotic Turkish retreat (page 120).

For the late Rudolph Nureyev, an antique copper tub with elaborate taps

took center stage in his fantasy bathroom (page 131). With a candelabra casting shadows and glow, it is a glorious, gilded room worthy of a Russian palace. Another glittering palace of a bathroom comes to life at the Hôtel de Beauharnais in Paris, where walls of mirrors endlessly reflect the beauty of its decorative surfaces (page 130).

In some fantasies the sense of touch predominates, and the bath becomes a wholly physical experience. The communion with nature offered by the bathrooms on pages 132 and 133, the promise of a steamy sauna in a rustic room (page 134), a glorious downspout on a city rooftop (page 135)—these are full-body baths that speak of physical release.

When it comes time to create your fantasy bathroom, indulge your secret desires. You might find yourself surrounded by neoclassical motifs in a Roman-style bath (page 128), or in a whimsical portholed room modeled after the great ocean liners (pages 124 and 125), or even in a glamorous Parisian room fit for the Duke and Duchess of Windsor (pages 6, 126, and 127).

Whatever your wildest fancy might be, the following rooms prove that dreams really do come true.

PAGES 116 AND 117

Have you ever dreamed of bathing in a private grotto? No modern-day mermaid or merman could resist this deep tub, fed by a lion's head and surrounded by a collection of shells from the seven seas. A curved wall of rough-textured stone blocks make it seem like a bathing cave carved out of a rocky coast.

Floral designer Kenneth Turner has brought the outdoors inside with an array of exotic plants. His exuberant garden imagery extends to the weathered stone capital sitting on the floor, suggesting a place of repose in an English garden, and twig baskets overflowing with petals and scents. An angled mirror on the wall reflects a sink area that blooms with bouquets of seashells. (LEFT)

A stolen glance into Kenneth Turner's adjoining bedroom reveals that he has indeed transformed his bathroom into a lush oasis. Note the earthenware teapot, the stacked woven storage baskets, tropical shells, and pumice stones, all of which suggest far-flung destinations— a tiny island in the China Sea, perhaps, or a secret garden in Bali. Even in less opulent environments, the same South Seas atmosphere can be re-created with oversized plants and many-textured baskets.

119

One thousand and one Arabian nights could be spent adrift in this magnificent Turkish bath. You needn't be a pasha to capture the mood, however; a round tub, overlapping arches, and twinkling-star lights can be enough to make the seductive fantasy come to life. (FACING PAGE)

When Christophe Gollut designed this London bathroom, he wanted his clients to feel as though they could be luxuriating on the Mediterranean. The trompe l'oeil mural, painted by Pierre-Marie Rudelle, features a fantasy landscape that turns bath time into dream time. (RIGHT)

121

Moroccans have a passion for water and ornamental pools, which throughout their history have been infused with religious meaning. Here, all the exoticism of a North African nobleman's house has been transported to England. A sunken tub and the surrounding walls are paved with tiles, while the rich terra-cotta paint evokes the Moroccan earth. A narrow stained-glass window, inspired by the mihrab niche, is mimicked by the shape that frames the shower head.

122

In the restored Shiwaniwas palace in Udaipur, India, carved doorways flank an expanse of diagonally set floor tiles. The look is mysterious, exotic, and not so difficult to re-create: with the addition of a custom-cut arch, the ambitious do-it-yourselfer could turn a mere entranceway into a magical threshold.

123

When Piers Gough of CZWG designed this loft bathroom for Andrew and Julie Wadsworth, he conjured up the age of grand ocean liners, posh staterooms, and champagne baths. Clean, geometric shapes prevail: circular "porthole" windows, a carved niche for a round Jacuzzi, and truncated-triangle mirrors all enhance the narrow space. (FACING PAGE)

It's shipboard romance: twin pedestal sinks each have their own inset arch with discrete shelving to hold bracing fragrances. Adding to this bathroom's unique style is the entranceway: swinging doors, curved at the top, feature frosted windows whose shape echoes the unusual geometry of the bathroom mirrors. Bon voyage. (RIGHT)

Oh, the fantasy of it all!
In the late Duchess of Windsor's
Paris bathroom, a platform tub,
a faux-tented ceiling, drawing
room furniture, and a fantastic
array of mirrors make an
environment that is part powder
room, part ladies' parlor, and
altogether enchanting.

126

Wallis Simpson was known for her romantic nature. It's evident here in candle-fitted sconces, a custom-made cabinet, a slipper chair with spiderweb upholstery and deep fringe, and a length of gauzy white curtains against a view of the garden. (ABOVE)

In the Duke and Duchess of Windsor's day, the idea that a bathroom could double as a sitting room was a cutting-edge concept. Also ahead of its time was the specially commissioned tentlike marquee and the images appliquéd on the walls. The furniture, inspired by eighteenth- and nineteenth-century models, was designed for her. (RIGHT)

127

It is known as the Atrium at the Roman Baths. With its massive marble tub and Pompeian red walls ornamented with classical figures posturing in pavilions, it looks like the palatial bath of an ancient emperor. In fact, it is a neoclassical dream: located in Potsdam, it was designed by Schinkel and Persius in the early nineteenth century, when tastes ran to all things neoclassical. (FACING PAGE)

Flanked by marble pillars and crowned with a vaulted ceiling, the majestic master bath in Manderston, a turn-of-the-century country house, is a veritable altar of bathing. (RIGHT)

Where to feast your eyes first?
The inlaid marble floor? The
carved bath surround? The slender
marble pillars? The patterned
ceiling? In this fantastic house
of mirrors in the Hôtel de
Beauharnais in Paris, every view
is a delirious reflection of color,
texture, and light.

130

A consummate collector, the late Rudolph
Nureyev transformed his apartments into
fantasy environments embellished with tiled,
painted, and gilded surfaces. Above, an
antique French copper tub glows against tiles
whose rich patterns look as though they were
lifted from a magic carpet. (ABOVE)

In another of Nureyev's bathrooms,
faux-finished walls play counterpoint to a
gilded ceiling, all bathed in candlelight.
A fantastic set of turn-of-the-century taps
and a luxurious ring shower comprise the
exotic waterworks. (RIGHT)

131

In true tropical climates there is always an open relationship between the outdoors and the indoors. This bathroom at the Sonera Fushi Hotel on one of the exotic Maldive Islands, in the Indian Ocean, is a lush example of that natural communion. In cooler climes, blooming plants in a window box, luscious potted foliage surrounding the tub, and cut blossoms perched on surfaces can go a long way toward creating a tropical fantasyland. An even greater effect can be achieved by covering walls with inexpensive stucco or plaster and adding imaginative touches, such as fish-shaped hooks, baskets, and terra-cotta pots. (LEFT)

Sheltered beneath a thatched roof, surrounded by sea-kissed air, this bathroom is both a serene retreat and a celebration of tropical beauty. When the blazing Maldivian sun begins to set, the room holds the promise of a civilized soak or a refreshing shower. In the morning it is the perfect place to sip tea and anticipate an exquisitely lazy beach day.

132

The sauna is a great Scandinavian tradition, and this rustic room, located in the late Eliel Saarinen's country house outside Helsinki, exemplifies classic sauna style. With simple wooden benches adjoined by a bare-basics shower, one can imagine how rejuvenating its intense heat would feel in deepest winter. An especially inviting aspect of this room is its split-log walls. If the idea of a cozy cabin appeals to you, why not consider covering your bathroom walls in rough, tough timber? (FACING PAGE)

On muggy August afternoons in the unrelenting heat of the city, millions of sweltering New Yorkers dream of relief. But how many can go home to a cooling deluge at the top of the world? With the sky above, rooftops all around, and nothing but a flood of icy water between you and the view, this is perhaps the urbanite's ultimate escape. (RIGHT)

135

SOURCES

1 3 6

UNITED STATES

*Department Stores /
General Furnishings and
Accessories Chains*

Bloomingdale's
Bullock's
Crate & Barrel
Dillard's
Ikea
Macy's
Neiman-Marcus
Saks Fifth Avenue
Stein Mart

Mail Order

L. L. Bean
Freeport, ME 04033
(800) 221-4221

Chambers
P.O. Box 7841
San Francisco, CA 94120
(800) 334-9790

The Company Store
500 Company Store Road
La Crosse, WI 54601-4477
(800) 323-8000

Crate & Barrel
P.O. Box 9059
Wheeling, IL 60090
(800) 323-5461
(708) 520-4747

Cuddledown of Maine
312 Canco Road
Portland, ME 04101
(800) 323-6793

Eddie Bauer Home
P.O. Box 3700
Seattle, WA 98124
(800) 426-8020

Garnet Hill
262 Main Street
Franconia, NH 03580
(800) 622-6216
(603) 823-5545

Hammacher Schlemmer
9180 Le Saint Drive
Fairfield, OH 45014
(800) 543-3366
(513) 860-4570

Hold Everything
Mail Order Department
P.O. Box 7807
San Francisco, CA 94120-
7807
(800) 421-2264

The Horchow Collection
P.O. Box 620048
Dallas, TX 75262-0048
(800) 456-7000
(214) 556-6000

Land's End "Coming Home"
Catalogue
1 Land's End Lane
Dept. FW
Dodgeville, WI 53595
(800) 356-4444

Paper White
P.O. Box 956
Fairfax, CA 94930
(800) 677-1991

Pottery Barn
100 North Point Street
San Francisco, CA 94133
(800) 922-5507

NEW YORK

*Department / General
Furnishings and
Accessories Stores*

ABC Carpet & Home
888 Broadway
(212) 473-3000

Barneys
660 Madison Avenue
(212) 826-8900
and branches

Bed, Bath and Beyond
620 Avenue of the Americas
(212) 255-3550

Bergdorf Goodman
754 Fifth Avenue
(212) 753-7300

Felissimo
10 West 56th Street
(212) 247-5656

Laura Ashley
714 Madison Avenue
(212) 735-5000

Portico Collection
379 West Broadway
(212) 941-7722

Zona
97 Greene Street
(212) 925-6750

Bathroom Showrooms

The Bath House
215 Thompson Street
(212) 533-0690

Davis & Warshow Inc.
A&D Showrooms
150 East 58th Street
(212) 688-5990

Gracious Home
1220 Third Avenue
(212) 517-6300

Hastings
230 Park Avenue South
(212) 674-9700

Kraft Hardware
306 East 61st Street
(212) 838-2214

Simon's Hardware
421 Third Avenue
(212) 532-9220

Sherle Wagner
60 East 57th Street
(212) 758-3300

M. Wolchonok & Son
155 East 52nd Street
(212) 755-2168

Flooring / Tiles

Country Floors
15 East 16th Street
(212) 627-8300

Nemo Tile
48 East 21st Street
(212) 505-0009

Ann Sacks Tile and Stone
5 East 16th Street
(212) 463-8400

Quarry Tile Marble and
Granite
192 Lexington Avenue
(212) 679-8889

Accessories

Calvin Klein
654 Madison Avenue
(212) 292-9000

Chartreuse
309 East 9th Street
(212) 254-8477

Cobweb Antique Imports
116 West Houston Street
(212) 505-1558

Linda Horn Antiques
1015 Madison Avenue
(212) 772-1122

William Hunrath Co.
153 East 57th Street
(212) 758-0780

Howard Kaplan Antiques
827 Broadway
(212) 674-1000

The Paris Apartment
324 and 328 East 9th Street
(212) 780-0232

Pierre Deux Fabrics
870 Madison Avenue
(212) 570-9343

Ralph Lauren
867 Madison Avenue
(212) 606-2100

Slatkin & Co.
131 East 70th Street
(212) 794-1661

Tiger's Eye Bed & Bath
157 West 72nd Street
(212) 496-8488

Waterworks
237 East 58th Street
(212) 371-9266
and branches

William Wayne & Co.
846-850 Lexington Avenue
(212) 737-8934
(212) 288-9243

Linens / Towels

Ad Hoc Softwares
410 West Broadway
(212) 925-2652

E. Braun & Co.
717 Madison Avenue
(212) 838-0650

Frette Linen
799 Madison Avenue
(212) 988-5221

Leron, Inc. Linen
750 Madison Avenue
(212) 753-6700

D. Porthault Inc.
18 East 69th Street
(212) 688-1660

Portico Bed and Bath
139 Spring Street
(212) 941-7722

Pratesi Linen Boutique
829 Madison Avenue
(212) 288-2315

Schweitzer Linens
457 Columbus Avenue;
1132 Madison Avenue;
1053 Lexington Avenue

Wolfman, Gold & Good
116 Greene Street
(212) 431-1888

Bath Products

GapScents
Gap
620 Avenue of the Americas
and branches

Robert Isabell
1-800-Isabell for deliveries

L'Artisan Parfumeur
870 Madison Avenue
(212) 517-8665

Architectural Salvage

Great American Salvage
Company
34 Cooper Square
(212) 505-0070

Irreplaceable Artifacts
14 Second Avenue
(212) 777-2900

Antiques Market

The Annex Antiques Fair &
Flea Market
Sixth Avenue from 24th to
28th Street

GREAT BRITAIN

Mail-Order Catalogues

Antique Designs
Penny Kempton
Orchard Farm
Brow Lane
Antrobus
Cheshire CW9 6JY
(0565) 777-376

Cologne & Cotton
74 Regent Street
Leamington Spa
Warwickshire CV32 4NS
(0926) 332-573

The White Company
298-300 Munster Road
London W6
(0171) 385-7988

LONDON AND ENVIRONS

Department / General Furnishings and Accessories Stores

The Conran Shop
The Michelin Building
81 Fulham Road, SW3

General Trading Company
144 Sloane Street, SW1

Habitat
196 Tottenham Court
Road, W1;
206 King's Road, SW3

Harrod's
Knightsbridge, SW1

Harvey Nichols
109-125 Knightsbridge,
SW1

Heal's
196 Tottenham Court
Road, W1;
234 King's Road, SW3

Ikea
2 Drury Way
North Circular Road, NW10

Jerry's Home Store
163-167 Fulham Road, SW3

John Lewis
278-306 Oxford Street, W1

Liberty
Regent Street, W1

Muji, No Brand Goods
26 Great Marlborough
Street, W1;
157 Kensington High
Street, W8

Peter Jones
Sloane Square, SW1

Selfridges
400 Oxford Street, W1

Bathroom Showrooms

Alternative Plans
9 Hester Road, SW11
(Contemporary made-to-
order bathrooms by
descendants of Thomas
Crapper, an inventor
of the flushing toilet)

Aston Matthews
141-147a Essex Road, N1

Bathroom City
Amington Road
Tysleley
Birmingham

Bathroom Discount Centre
297 Munster Road
Fulham, SW6 6BW

The Bathroom Store
75 Upper Richmond Road
Putney, London SW15
and branches

Burge & Gunson
13-23 High Street
Colliers Wood, SW19

Chadder & Co.
Bleinham Studio
Forest Row
East Sussex R17 8SEZ

Colour Wash
63-65 Fulham High Street,
SW6 3IJ
and branches

Czech & Speake
39C Jermyn Street, SW1;
125 Fulham Road, SW3

C. P. Hart
Newnham Terrace
Hercules Road, SE1

Ideal Standard
The Bathroom Works
Hull HU5 4HS

Matki Finesse
(01454) 322 888

M&O Bathroom Centre
174-176 Goswell Road,
EC1V 7DT

Original Bathrooms
143-145 Kew Road
Richmond, Surrey
(Run by descendants of
Thomas Crapper's
apprentice Frederick
Humpherson)

Max Pike Bathrooms
4 Eccleston Street, SW1

Pipe Dreams
72 Gloucester Road, SW7

Sitting Pretty
131 Dawes Road, SW6

Smallbone of Devizes
Fulham Road, SW3

West One Bathrooms Ltd.
60 Queenstown Road,
SW8 3RY

Period-Style Bathrooms / Restyled Fittings / Re-Enameling

Alscot Bathroom Company
Stratford-on-Avon WO1
(01789) 450-861
Friday, Saturday, and Sunday
by appointment

Bath Craft
(01722) 338999

The Bath Doctor
Prospect House
Canterbury Road
Challock, Ashford A252

Bathshield
(0342) 823-243

Drummonds of Bramley
Birtley Farm
Horsham Road
Bramley-near-Guildford
Surrey

Old-Fashioned Bathrooms
Little London Hill
Debenham
Suffolk IP14 6PW

The Original Period Bath
Company
39 Potovens Lane
Lofthouse Gate
Wakefield
(01924) 824-246

Posh Tubs
Little London Hill
Debenham
Suffolk IP14 6PW

Roll Top Baths Galore
(0700) 04422847

Tosca & Willoughby
Home Farm
Aston Bowant

Water Monopoly
16-18 Lonsdale Road, NW6
(Restoration of antique
and period bathrooms and
sanitary ware)

Mary Rose Young
Bathrooms
Oak House, Arthur's Folly
Parkend, Lidney,
Gloucestershire GL15 4JQ
(01594) 5534225

Flooring / Tiles

Crucial Trading, Ltd.
77 Westbourne Park
Road, W2
and branches
(Natural flooring)

Dalsouple Flooring
P.O. Box 140
Bridgewater
Somerset TA5 1HT
(Rubber flooring)

Fired Earth
Twyford Mill
Oxford Road
Adderbury
Oxon OX17 3HP

Paris Ceramics, Ltd.
583 King's Road, SW6 2EH

The Reject Tile Shop
178 Wandsworth Bridge
Road, SW6

World's End Tiles
9 Langton Street, SW10

Accessories

The Blue Door
77 Church Road, SW13

Maryse Boxer and Carolyn
Quartermaine
Chez Joseph
26 Sloane Street, SW1

Nina Campbell
9 Walton Street, SW3

Cath Kidston Ltd.
8 Clarendon Cross, W11
4AP

Chalon
The Plaza
535 King's Road, SW10 0SZ
(Painted furniture suitable
for storage)

Jane Churchill
151 Sloane Street, SW1

Colefax and Fowler
39 Brook Street, W1;
110 Fulham Road, SW3

Designers Guild
267 & 277 King's Road,
SW3

The Dormy House
Stirling Park
East Portway Industrial
Estate
Andover
Hants SP10 3TZ
(Made-to-order dressing
tables, etc.)

Pierre Frey
253 Fulham Road, SW3

Glass Blocks
Luxcrete
(0181) 965-7292

Christophe Gollut
116 Fulham Road, SW3

Judy Greenwood Antiques
657 Fulham Road, SW6

Nicholas Haslam
12 Holbein Place, SW1

The Holding Company
243-245 King's Road, SW3

Stephanie Hoppen
Decorative Pictures
17 Walton Street, SW3

H.R.W. Antiques
4a King's Avenue, SW4

Les Olivades
7 Walton Street, SW3

David Linley Furniture,
Ltd.
60 Pimlico Road, SW1

Looking Glass of Bath
94-96 Walcot Street
Bath BA1 5BG

The Manor Bindery
Fawley, Hampshire SO45
1BB
(Faux books for cupboards,
etc.)

Mrs. Monro
16 Motcomb Street, SW1

Christopher Moore
Antique Textiles
1 Munro Terrace
Cheyne Walk, SW10

Mulberry
41/42 New Bond Street,
W1

W.H. Newson Hardware
61 Pimlico Road, SW1

Osborne and Little
304 King's Road, SW3

Port of Call, Ltd.
13 Walton Street, SW3

Ralph Lauren Home
Collection
Harvey Nichols, Harrod's
House of Fraser, Selfridges

George Spencer
Designs Ltd.
4 West Halkin Street, SW1

John Stefanidis
261 Fulham Road, SW3

Timney-Fowler
388 King's Road, SW3

Universal Providers
86 Golborne Road, W10

Valerie Wade
108 Fulham Road, SW3

Nicola Wingate-Saul
Print Rooms
43 Moreton Street, SW1

Joanna Wood Ltd.
48A Pimlico Road, SW3

William Yeoward
336 King's Road, SW35 UR

Linens / Towels

Elizabeth Baer
Pavilion Antiques
Freshford Hall
Freshford
Nr. Bath
Avon BA3 6EJ

Claridge & Co.
154 Wandsworth Bridge
Road, SW6

Damask
3-4 Broxholme House
New King's Road, SW6

J&M Davidson
62 Ledbury Road, W11

Descamps
197 Sloane Street, SW1

Frette
98 New Bond Street, W1

Givan's Irish Linen Store
207 King's Road, SW3

Irish Linen Co.
35 Burlington Arcade, W1

The Linen Merchant
11 Montpelier Street, SW7

The Monogrammed Linen
Shop
168 Walton Street, SW3

Le Tissus Français
227 Ebury Street, SW1

The White House
51/52 New Bond Street,
W1

Yves De Lorme at Liberty
(see Liberty/Dept. Stores)

Bath Products

Crabtree and Evelyn
234 King's Road, SW3

Culpepper
21 Bruton Street
Berkeley Square, W1

Floris
89 Jermyn Street, SW1

GapScents
Gap
122 King's Road, SW3 4TR;
208 Regent Street, W1R
7DD;
and branches

L'Artisan Parfumeur
17 Cale Street, SW3

Jo Malone
154 Walton Street, SW3 2JL

Molton Brown
58 South Molton Street,
W1H 1YY

Penhaligon's
41 Wellington Street, WC2

Santa Maria Novella
117 Walton Street, SW3

Architectural Salvage

Architectural Salvage
Register (Index of salvage
dealers and items)
(0483) 203 221

Crowthers of Syon
Lodge Ltd.
Syon Lodge
Busch Corner
London Road
Isleworth, Middlesex
TW7 5BH

The House Hospital
68 Battersea High Street,
SW11

LassCo Architectural
Antique Salvage
Mark Street
(off Paul Street), EC2

The Period House
Dept. MB
Main Street
Leavening, N. Yorks
YO17 95
(0585) 87383

Salvo
1 The Cottage
Ford Woodhouse Farm
Berwick-Upon-Tweed
TD15 2QF
(01225) 445387

Walcot Reclamation
108 Walcot Street
Bath
Avon BA1 5BG

Open-Air Antiques
Markets

Bermondsey
Bermondsey Square and
Tower Bridge Road, SE1

Camden Passage
Islington, N1

Portobello Road, W11

Indoor Antiques Markets

Antiquarius Antique Market
131 King's Road, SW3

Chenil Galleries
181-183 King's Road, SW3

Gray's Antique Market
58 Davies Street, W1

General Information

The Essential Bathroom
Guide
The Bathroom Showroom
Association
Freepost, Dept. HAG/3,
Federation House
Stoke-on-Trent ST4 2BR

FRANCE

PARIS AND ENVIRONS

Department / General
Furnishings and
Accessories Stores

BHV
52 rue de Rivoli, 75004

Le Bon Marché
22 rue de Sèvres, 75007

The Conran Shop
117 rue du Bac, 75007
and branches

138

Galeries Lafayette
40 bd Haussmann, 75009

Habitat
17 rue de l'Arrivée, 75014

Ikea
202 rue Henri Barbosse,
78370 Plaisir

Printemps Haussmann
64 bd Haussmann, 75009

Samaritaine
19 rue de la Monnaie,
75001

Bathroom Showrooms

Allia Showroom
44 rue Berger, 75001

Aux Bains Dallançon
20 rue Benjamin-Franklin,
75016

Bains Plus
51 rue des Francs-
Bourgeois, 75004

Bath Shop
3 rue Gros, 75016

Cascade
7A bd Richard-Lenoir,
75011

C.E.D.E.O.
74 bd Richard-Lenoir,
75011

Jean-Claude D'Armant
La Griffe du Bain
79 av Ledru-Rollin, 75012

Jacob Delafon
(331) 40-27-5300 (for list
of showrooms)

J. Delepine
104 bd de Clichy, 75018

Porcelaine de Paris
13 rue de La Pierre Levée,
75011

Porcher
16 place de la Madeleine;
63 rue Billancourt
Boulogne

Séraphin
20 rue de la Folie-
Méricourt, 75011

Sophia Industries
44 rue Blanche, 75009

Villeroy et Boch
82 rue d'Hauteville, 75010

Period-Style Bathrooms / Re-Enameling

A L'Epi d'Or
17 rue des Bernadins,
75005

Didier Maraut
Marche Serpette, stand 5,
alle 3—Puces de Saint-
Ouen
93400 Saint-Ouen

En D'Autres Thermes
4 rue Saint-Sabin, 75011

La Baignoire Délirante
26 rue de Lourmel, 75015

Le Bain Rose
11 rue d'Assas, 75006

Protocabain
63 rue de Billancourt
92100 Boulogne

Saponifère
59 rue Bonaparte, 75006

Accessories

Beauté Divine
40 rue Saint Sulpice, 75006

Biggie Best
28 rue Saint-Sulpice, 75006;
9/11 rue des Lavandières
Saint-Opportune, 75001

Boutique Elle
30 rue Saint-Sulpice, 75006

Braquenié
111 bd Beaumarchais,
75003

Manuel Canovas
5 place Furstenberg, 75006

Comoglio Paris
22 rue Jacob, 75006

Etamine
63 rue du Bac, 75007

Patrick Frey
47 rue des Petits Champs,
75001;
5 rue Jacob, 75006

Garouste et Bonetti
through Galerie Neotu
25 rue du Renard, 75004

Laura Ashley
261 rue Saint-Honoré,
75001

Maison de Famille
29 rue Saint-Sulpice, 75006

Marie-Christine de la
Rochefoucauld
16 rue de l'Université,
75007

Mlinaric, Henry and
Zervudachi
54 galerie de Montpensier,
75001

Nobilis-Fontan
29 rue Bonaparte, 75006

Noblesse Oblige
27 bis, rue de Bellechasse,
75007

Ralph Lauren Home
Collection
2 place de la Madeleine,
75008

Souleiado
83 av Paul Doumer, 75016

Linens / Towels

La Boutique du Sommeil
24 av Pierre-1er-de-Serbie,
75016

Carré Blanc
33 rue de Sèvres, 75006;
111 bis, rue de Courcelles,
75017

Casa Caïada
12 rue Jacob, 75006

La Chatelaine
170 av Victor Hugo, 75016

Chiff-Tir
20 av des Ternes, 75017

Agnès Comar S.A.
7 av Georges V, 75008

Yves Delorme
153 rue Saint-Honoré,
75001

Anaïk Descamps
at Galeries Lafayette
40 bd Haussmann, 75009

Boutique Descamps
44 rue de Passy, 75016;
38 rue du Four, 75006;
and branches

Descamps Michel Ange
Auteuil
4 rue Donizetti, 75016

Olivier Desforges
26 bd Raspail, 75007;
8 av Mozart, 75016

Christian Dior
32 av Montaigne, 75008

Frette
48 faubourg Saint-Honoré,
75008

Muriel Grateau Boutique
Maison
132-133 galerie de Valois,
75001

Yves Halard
252 bis, bd Saint-Germain,
75007

Kenzo
3 place des Victoires, 75001

La Maison de Renata
2 bd Raspail, 75007

Matins Bleus
92 rue de Rennes, 75006

Catherine Memmi
32-34 rue Saint-Sulpice,
75006

Nouez-Moi
27 rue des Sablons, 75016

Nuit Blanche
41 rue de Bourgogne,
75007

La Paresse en Douce
97 rue du Bac, 75007

Porthault
18 av Montaigne, 75008

Nina Ricci
39 av Montaigne, 75008

Le Trefle Bleu
2 rue Largillière, 75016

Bath Products

Annick Goutal
14 rue de Castiglione,
75001

Crabtree and Evelyn
177 bd Saint Germain,
75007

Diptyque
34 bd Saint Germain, 75005

Grain de Beauté
9 rue du Cherche-Midi,
75006

Herboristerie du Palais-
Royal
11 rue des Petits Champs,
75001

Jean-François Laporte
84 bis, rue de Grenelle,
75007

P. de Nicolaii
80 rue de Grenelle, 75007

Markets

Le Village Saint-Paul
rue Saint Paul, 75004

Le Village Suisse
54 av de la Motte Piquet,
75007

Les marchés aux puces:
Clignancourt; St.-Ouen;
Vanves; Montreuil

Marché Didot
Porte de Vanves

PROVENCE

Accessories

Michel Biehn
7 av des Quatre-Otages
84800 L'Isle-Sur-La-Sorgue

Edith Mézard
Château de l'Ange
84220 Lumières
(linens)

Les Olivades
28 rue Lafayette
13210 St. Rémy-de-
Provence
and branches

Musée Souleiado
39 rue Proudhon
13150 Tarascon

Souleiado
2 av de la Résistance
13210 St. Rémy-de-
Provence
and branches

Xavier Nicod
9 av des Quatres-Otages
L'Isle-Sur-La-Sorgue
(Period bathroom
accessories)

Bath Products

Les Coquineries d'Eso
La Boutique
43 bd Victor Hugo
13210 Saint-Remy-de-
Provence

L'Herbier de Provence
La Santoline
bd Victor Hugo
13210 Saint-Remy-de-
Provence

Antiques Market

L'Isle-Sur-La-Sorgue
(Sunday mornings)

ITALY

MILAN

Bathroom Showrooms

Aqua Tech
Via Vincenzo Monti, 2

Crave
Viale Dell'Industria

Crovato
Piazza Guardi, 4

La Casa Del Bagno
Viale Monza, 237

Savioli
Via B/Duttinoni, 3

*Linens/Towels/
Accessories*

MILAN

Bassetti
Corso Garibaldi, 20

Frette
Via Visconti di Modrone 15;
Corso Buenos Aires 82;
Corso Vercelli 23/25;
Via Torino 42

Mirabello
Via Montebello (corner of
Via San Marco)

Pratesi
Via Montenapoleone 27/B

Sogaro
Corso di Porta Romana, 40

ROME

Frette
Viale Libia 192;
Via del Corso 381;
Via Nazionale 84

VENICE

Jesurum
Ponte Canonica 4310

Martinuzzi
San Marco, 67

Pistoia
Pratesi S.p.A.-
Direct Factory Sales
Località Ponte Stella
51034 Pistoia

SELECTED BIBLIOGRAPHY

Agius, Pauline. Introduction to Stephen Jones. *Ackermann's Regency Furniture and Interiors.* Marlborough: The Crowood Press, 1984.

Ariès, Philippe, and Georges Duby, general editors. *A History of Private Life: Vol. 3. Passions of the Renaissance.* Translated by Arthur Goldhammer. Cambridge, Mass.: The Belknap Press of Harvard University Press, 1989.

Barwick, Jo Ann, and Norma Skurka. *Scandinavian Country.* New York: Clarkson Potter, 1991.

Beard, Geoffrey. *Craftsmen and Interior Decoration in England, 1660–1820.* London: John Bartholomew and Son, 1981; London: Bloomsbury Books, 1986.

———. *The National Trust Book of the English House Interior.* London: Viking, 1990.

Becker, Robert. *Nancy Lancaster: Her Life, Her World, Her Art.* New York: Alfred A. Knopf, 1996.

Braudel, Fernand. Translated by Sian Reynolds. *The Structures of Everyday Life: Civilization and Capitalism 15th–18th Century. The Limits of the Possible.* New York: Harper & Row, 1979.

Brédit, Josette. *Classic Printed Textiles from France, 1760–1843, Toiles de Jouy.* Paris: Editions Adam Biro, 1989. London: Thames and Hudson, 1989.

Briggs, Asa. *Victorian Things.* London: B. T. Batsford, Ltd., 1988.

Bruce, Evangeline. *Napoleon and Josephine: An Improbable Marriage.* London: Weidenfeld & Nicholson, 1995.

Campbell, Nina, and Caroline Seebohm. *Elsie de Wolfe: A Decorative Life.* New York: Panache Press, 1992.

Chambers, James. *The English House.* London: Methuen London, Ltd., 1985.

Charles-Roux, Edmonde. Translated by Nancy Amphoux. *Chanel: Her Life, Her World, and the Woman Behind the Legend She Herself Created.* New York: Alfred A. Knopf, 1975.

Chippendale, Thomas. *The Gentleman and Cabinet-Maker's Director.* Reprint of 3d ed., 1762. New York: Dover Publications, 1966.

Christie's, *Nureyev,* Part I. Sale Catalogue. New York: Christie's Publications, 1995.

Christie's, *Nureyev,* Part II. Sale Catalogue. London: Christie's Publications, 1995.

Collard, Frances. *Regency Furniture.* Woodbridge, Suffolk, England: Antique Collectors' Club, 1985.

Cruickshank, Dan, and Neil Burton. *Life in the Georgian City.* London: Viking, 1990.

Davidson, Caroline. *Women's Worlds: The Art and Life of Mary Ellen Best, 1809–1891.* Foreword by Howard Rutkowski. New York: Crown Publishers, 1985.

De Bonneville, Françoise. Preface by Marc Porthault.

Translated by Deke Dusinberre. *The Book of Fine Linen.* Paris: Flammarion, 1994.

Douglas, Mary T., and Baron Isherwood. *The World of Goods.* New York: Basic Books, 1979.

Du Prey, Pierre de la Ruffinière. *Sir John Soane.* London: Victoria and Albert Museum, 1985.

Eastlake, Charles L. New Introduction by John Gloag. *Hints on Household Taste. The Classic Handbook of Victorian Interior Decoration.* New York: Dover Publications, 1969. Originally published in 1878.

Fowler, John, and John Cornforth. *English Decoration in the Eighteenth Century.* London: Barrie and Jenkins, 1986.

Garrett, Elisabeth Donaghy. *At Home: The American Family, 1750–1870.* New York: Harry N. Abrams, 1990.

Gere, Charlotte. *Nineteenth-Century Decoration: The Art of the Interior.* London: Weidenfeld and Nicolson, 1989.

Gilliam, Jan Kirsten, and Betty Crowe Leviner. *Furnishing Williamsburg's Historic Buildings.* Williamsburg, Va.: Colonial Williamsburg Foundation, 1991.

Girouard, Mark. *A Country House Companion.* New Haven and London: Yale University Press, 1987.

———. *Life in the English Country House.* New Haven and London: Yale University Press, 1978; Harmondsworth, Middlesex, England, and New York: Penguin Books, 1980.

Groth, Håkan. *Neoclassicism in the North: Swedish Furniture and Interiors, 1770–1800.* London: Thames and Hudson, 1990.

Heal, Sir Ambrose. *London Furniture Makers 1660–1840.* London: Butler and Tanner, Ltd., 1988.

Hepplewhite, George. *The Cabinet-Maker and Upholsterer's Guide.* Introduction by Joseph Aronson. Reprint of 3d ed., 1794. New York: Dover Publications, 1969.

Heskett, John. *Industrial Design.* New York and Toronto: Oxford University Press, 1980.

Jackson-Stops, Gervase, and James Pipkin. *The English Country House: A Grand Tour.* London: Weidenfeld and Nicolson, and The National Trust, 1985.

Johnson, Lorraine, and Gabrielle Townsend. *Osborne and Little: The Decorated Room.* Exeter, Devon: Webb and Bower, Ltd., 1988.

Jones, Chester. *Colefax and Fowler.* London: Barrie and Jenkins, 1989.

Lambton, Lucinda. *Temples of Convenience and Chambers of Delight.* London: Pavilion Books, 1995. (First published in 1978.)

Lewis, Lady Theresa, ed. *Extracts of the Journals and Correspondence of Miss Berry, 1783–1852.* Vols. 1–3. London: Longmans, Green and Co., 1865.

Lucie-Smith, Edward. *Furniture: A Concise History.* New York and Toronto: Oxford University Press, 1979.

McKendrick, Neil, John Brewer, and J. H. Plumb. *The Birth of a Consumer Society: The Commercialization of Eighteenth-Century England.* Bloomington: Indiana University Press, 1982.

Mitford, Mary Russell. *Our Village: Sketches of Rural Character and Scenery.* Vols. 1–2. Paris: Baudry's European Library, 1839.

Mitford, Nancy. *Madame de Pompadour.* London: Hamish Hamilton, 1988. (First published in 1954.)

Montgomery, Florence. *Textiles in America 1650–1870.* New York: W. W. Norton and Co., 1984.

Morley, John. *Regency Design 1790–1840.* London: A. Zwemmer, Ltd., 1793.

Moseley, Charlotte, ed. *The Letters of Nancy Mitford.* London: Hodder & Stoughton, 1993.

Mott, George, and Sally Sample Aall. *Follies and Pleasure Pavilions.* Introduction by Gervase Jackson-Stops. London: Pavilion Books, 1989.

Nylander, Richard C., Elizabeth Redmond, and Penny J. Sander. *Wallpaper in New England.* Boston: Society for the Preservation of New England Antiquities, 1986.

Parissien, Steven. *Adam Style.* London: Phaidon Press, 1992.

———. *Regency Style.* London: Phaidon Press, 1992.

Praz, Mario. *An Illustrated History of Interior Decoration from Pompeii to Art Nouveau.* London: Thames and Hudson, 1964.

Rêves d'Alcôves: La Chambre au Cours de Siècles. Paris: Union Centrale des Arts Décoratifs—Réunion des Musées Nationaux, 1995.

Reyburn, Wallace. *Flushed With Pride: The Story of Thomas Crapper.* London: Pavilion Books, 1989. (First published by Macdonald and Company in 1969.)

Roberts, Robert. Foreword by Charles A. Hammond. *The House Servant's Directory.* Waltham, Mass.: The Gore Place Society, n.d. Facsimile of the 1827 edition.

Rosomon, Treve. *London Wallpapers: Their Manufacture and Use, 1690–1840.* London; English Heritage, 1992.

Rothstein, Natalie. *Silk Designs of the Eighteenth Century in the Collection of the Victoria and Albert Museum.* London: Thames and Hudson and the Board of Trustees of the Victoria and Albert Museum, 1990.

Rybczynski, Witold. *Home: A Short History of an Idea.* New York: Viking Penguin, 1986.

Saumarez Smith, Charles. *Eighteenth-Century Decoration: Design and the Domestic Interior in England.* London: Weidenfeld and Nicolson, 1993.

Savot, Louis. *L'Architecture Française.*

Schama, Simon. *The Embarrassment of Riches: An Interpretation of Dutch Culture in the Golden Age.* New York: Alfred A. Knopf, 1987.

Sheraton, Thomas. *The Cabinet-Maker and Upholsterer's Drawing Book.* Introduction by Joseph Aronson. Reprint of various early eds., 1793–1802. New York: Dover Publications, 1972.

Shoeser, Mary, and Celia Rufy. *English and American Textiles.* London: Thames and Hudson, 1989.

Simpson, James B., compiler. Foreword by Daniel J. Boorstin. *Simpson's Contemporary Quotations.* Boston: Houghton Mifflin Company, 1988.

Snodin, Michael. *Karl Friederich Schinkel: A Universal Man.* New Haven and London: Yale University Press in association with the Victoria and Albert Museum, 1991.

Thornton, Peter. *Authentic Decor: The Domestic Interior, 1620–1920.* New York: Viking, 1984.

———. *The Italian Renaissance Interior, 1400–1600.* London: Weidenfeld and Nicolson, 1991.

———. *Seventeenth-Century Interior Decoration in England, France and Holland.* New Haven and London: Yale University Press, 1978.

Townsend, Gabrielle, and Lorraine Johnson. *Osborne & Little: The Decorated Room.* London: Webb & Bower, 1988.

Troide, Lars E., ed. *The Early Journals and Letters of Fanny Burney 1768–1773.* Oxford: Clarendon Press, 1988.

———. *The Early Journals of Fanny Burney 1774–1777.* Oxford: Clarendon Press, 1990.

Vickers, Hugo. *The Private World of the Duke and Duchess of Windsor.* London: Harrod's Publishing, 1995; New York: Abbeville Press, 1996.

Von Furstenburg, Diane. *The Bath.* New York: Random House, 1993.

Vreeland, Diana. *DV.* Plimpton, George, and Christopher Hemphill, eds. New York: Alfred A. Knopf, 1984.

Ward-Jackson, Peter. *English Furniture Designs of the Eighteenth Century.* London: Victoria and Albert Museum, 1984.

Watkins, Susan. *Jane Austen's Town and Country Style.* London: Thames and Hudson, 1990; New York:

Rizzoli, 1990.

Wharton, Edith. Introduction by Marilyn French. *The Custom of the Country*. New York: Berkley in arrangement with Charles Scribner's Sons, 1981.

————. *The House of Mirth*. New York: Berkley Books, 1981.

Whatman, Susanna. Edited by Thomas Balston. *The Housekeeping Book of Susanna Whatman 1776–1800*. London: G. Bles, 1956.

White, Elizabeth. *Pictorial Dictionary of British Eighteenth-Century Furniture Design*. Woodbridge, Suffolk, England:

Antique Collectors Club, 1990.

Woolf, Virginia. *Mrs. Dalloway*. Published by Leonard and Virginia Woolf. London: The Hogarth Press, 1925.

Wright, Lawrence. *Clean and Decent: The Fascinating History of the Bathroom and the Water Closet*. London: Routledge and Kegan Paul, 1960.

Shopping Guides

Brabec, Dominique and Eglé Salvy. *Paris Chic: The Parisian's Own Insider Shopping Guide*. London: Thames

and Hudson, 1993.

Coté Sud. Nos Bonnes Addresses 94–95.

Gershman, Suzy. *Born to Shop: Italy*. New York: Harper-Collins, 1993.

————. *Born to Shop: New York,* 3d edition. New York: Bantam, 1990.

Guisez, Corinne, and Sylvie Tardrew. *Elle Deco: Le Carnet d'adresses*. Le Guide Hachette de la Decoration. Paris: Hachette, 1995.

The World of Interiors Decoration Dictionary: 1000 Vital Addresses, Part 1: A–F; Part 2: G–Z, 1996.

ACKNOWLEDGMENTS

I would like to express my sincerest thanks to everyone who participated in this project. I offer special thanks to everyone at Abbeville for their enthusiastic commitment to the series, especially Robert E. Abrams, President and Publisher, for his continuing support; Mark Magowan, for his imaginative ideas, encouragement, and treasured friendship; my editor, Jacqueline Decter, for her enthusiasm, delicious wit, and insightful, razor-sharp editing; Molly Shields, for her exquisite design; Lou Bilka; Jennifer Pierson; Susan Fletcher; Paula Trotto; Katie Kahn; and Myrna Smoot. I would also like to thank Marike Gauthier and her staff at Editions Abbeville, Paris, for all their help. Special thanks as well to John R. Murray, Nicholas Perren, Stephanie Allen, Helen Davis, Bridget Moon, and the rest of the staff at John Murray Publishers, London, for all their efforts on my behalf in Great Britain.

Special thanks to photographer Fritz von der Schulenburg, for his innate sense of style and instantaneous "interior vision"; he has been a delight to work with. And to Karen Howes of the Interior Archive for supplying credit information for all the photographs in the book, and for her continued friendship. I extend my great appreciation to the other photographers who contributed to this book, including Simon Brown, Tim Clinch, James Mortimer, Christopher Simon Sykes, and Henry Wilson.

Extra special thanks go to Todd Lyon, manuscript editor, for all her hard work, sensitivity, and telegraphic understanding of my ideas and writing style. Her cheerful attitude made it a pleasure to work with her.

Special thanks to Min Hogg, editor in chief of *The World of Interiors,* to whom I am forever indebted for "introducing" me to the London world of design. At *The World of Interiors* I would also like to thank Elfreda Pownall, Joan Hecktermann, Rupert Thomas, Annabel Freyberg, Samantha Body, and Dinah Hall.

Many thanks to Susan Crewe, editor in chief of *British House & Garden,* for her inspirational advice; Joanna Watt; Leonie Highton; and Anne Hardy, one of my closest friends, who provided indispensable advice, laughter, and support, always at the appropriate times.

Special thanks also to Clare Weatherall, editor in chief of *Period Living* and

Deborah Barker, formerly at the magazine; Lucia Von Der Post at the *Financial Times;* Tina Moran at the style section of the *Sunday Times,* London; June Ducas; Nikki Spencer at "The Big Breakfast," for inviting me to appear on the show; Deborah Wald of *Women's Journal; Architektur und Wohnen;* Radio Bristol of the BBC; and all the other journalists, too numerous to mention, who have been incredibly supportive.

Extra special thanks to David Green, chairman of Colefax and Fowler, who hosted the launch of *The Dining Room;* Ann Grafton; Trudi Ballard, director of public relations and a dear friend; Roger Banks-Pye; Tom Parr; Imogen Taylor; Pierre Serrurier; Lady Vivian Greenock; Becky Streeter; Emma Burns; and the entire team of decorators and staff, who not only helped with this project but have been wonderfully supportive of the whole series. Thanks also to Sibyl Colefax and John Fowler, and to social editor Celestia Noel for beautifully covering the launch party.

My sincerest thanks to all those who contributed their houses or their designs to this book. Although too numerous to mention here, they know who they are.

To David Llewellyn, whose wonderful stories of Rudolph Nureyev's apartments were fascinating; John Hardy; Meredith Etherington-Smith; and the Press Office, Christie's, London; and to Joe Friedman at Sotheby's, whose extensive information about the Duke and Duchess of Windsor was riveting. Special thanks to Mr. Mohamed Al Fayed, Christiane Sherwen and her staff at Harrod's Publishing, and the Al Fayed Archive for providing permission to include the pictures of the Duke and Duchess of Windsor's Parisian home.

To die-hard "shop-til-you-drop" shoppers and great friends Linda Costamagna, Lisa Eastman, Isabella Invernizzi, Patricia Pera, Judy Nyquist, Peter Ayers-Tarantino, and Julia Widdowson for their help in preparing the list of sources.

To David Mlinaric of Mlinaric, Henry & Zervudachi; Annabel Radermacher; Anouska Hempel; Siobahn Brown; Gearoid Cronin; Blakes Hotel; Nina Campbell; Sir Peter and Lady Osborne and Antony Little of Osborne & Little; Heather Ogie, GapScents, at Lynne Franks Public Relations; Donatella Pellini; Claire Usher at Stephanie Churchill Public Relations; Mr. François R. Touzin at Claridge's; Tessa Kennedy for her work at Claridge's; Kam Wong; the Savoy Group of Hotels and Restaurants; Miss E. Wesson.

To Colin Orchard and William Yeoward; Sally Metcalfe of George Spencer Designs; Christophe Gollut; Baldassare La Rizza; André de Cacqueray; Anne Boyd; Nico Rensch; Kenneth Turner; Piers Gough of CZWG; Lord Palmer of Manderston; Viscount Linley; Stephanie Hoppen; Designer's Guild; Elsa Peretti; Andrew and Julie Wadsworth; Nicholas Haslam; Wendy Harrop; Robert Nadler; Joanne Creveling; the Chanel Boutique; Paola Navone; Peter Wood & Partners; Joanna Wood; Charlotte Heneage; Cath Kidston; Christopher Gibbs; Mark Birley; the Halkin Hotel; Veuve Clicquot; Valentino; Andrea de Montal; Nick Maddison of Bibendum; Mimmi O'Connell of Port of Call; John Stefanidis and his staff, including Bruce Armstrong; André Heller; Count Heinrich Spreti; Child Graddon Lewis; Jerry Welling; Regalian Properties; Bingham Land; Karl Lagerfeld; Richard Mudditt; Laura Ashley; The Georgian Group; Glynn Boyd Harte; Sandra Ankarcrona of Coxe Design; Renzo Mongiardino; Jacques Granges; Stephen Woodhams; Christopher Moore Antique Textiles, not only for constructing an extraordinary bed in a London tent on a rainy evening for the launch of *The Bedroom,* but for knowing exactly how and when to indulge my love of toile de Jouy; Mr. Pidgeon of Original Bathrooms; the Flower Van; the Manhattan Loft Company; the Water Monopoly; Colour Wash; Chris Casson Madden; Cheryl MacLachlan; the Royal Oak Foundation; the National Trust; Dr. Neil Bingham at the Royal Institute of British Architects; Suzanne Colson and Victoria Timberlake at the Victoria and Albert Museum; Wendy Cooper at Winterthur; Susan Stein at Monticello; Barbara Carson, my thesis director, who started me off on the path to material culture; and Mary Herrmann and Martin Puris.

During my course of study, several authors have had a profound influence on my thinking, including Peter Thornton, Mark Girouard, Witold Rybczynski, Mary Douglas, and Baron Isherwood. If anyone's name has been

INDEX